Our Story
The Lives and Legacy of Those Who Served in Battery B First Rhode Island Light Artillery

Stephen G. Evangelista

Copyright © 2021
Stephen G. Evangelista
All rights reserved.
ISBN:

For Adriana, Sophia, and Nicholas
With Love

CONTENTS

	Introduction	2-5
1	Alfred G. Gardner	6
2	John Greene	16
3	Samuel Goldsmith	22
4	David B. King	28
5	David B. Patterson	32
6	Amos H. Armington	36
7	William Dennis	40
8	Albert Morris	44
9	William S. Perrin	50
10	Napoleon B. Clarke	56
11	John T. Blake	62
12	Edwin H. Knowles	68
13	John F. Leach	72
14	Thomas F. Brown	76
15	Eben S. Crowningshield	84
16	Joseph S. Milne	88
17	John E. Wardlow	92
18	Charles A. Brown	96
19	George McGunnigle	102
20	Gamaliel L. Dwight	108
21	Joseph S. Cassen	114
22	John G. Hazard	118
23	Charles A. Bowden	124
24	James McGunnigle	128
25	Gideon Spencer	132
26	The Matteson Brothers	138
27	David H. Phetteplace	144
28	John Delevan	148
29	Caleb H.H. Greene	154
30	James Blade	158
31	Robert A. Laird	162
32	Albert A. Straight	168
33	Charles D. Worthington	180
34	Henry H. Ballou	184
35	Stillman H. Budlong	188
36	John H. Rhodes	194
37	Levi J. Cornell	198
38	Albert J. Whipple	202
39	John Mahoney	206
40	Charles T. Straight	214
	Epilogue	220

Our Story

Battery B First Rhode Island Light Artillery Inc. Guidon

INTRODUCTION

One thing I know for certain, I love storytelling especially when the story is true. Perhaps that explains my love for history and its endless expanse of an unfolding narrative. I love how history has a unique way of intermingling with the present sometimes gently other times, with brute force. There is no more explicit example of how history reaches into the present than our American Civil War. Yet ever since I began to read and explore the many facets of this conflict, I have struggled with the challenge of having inadequate time (and the limited attention of those around me) to convey the depth and detail needed to fully understand this cataclysmic event.

Like so many other history enthusiasts, I have studied many books on the Civil War, watched numerous documentaries, and walked many battlefields. I have also tried to memorize facts and figures, the timeline of events, the generals and officers' names and, 1,001 other things in order to attempt to understand the inherent complexity and breadth of the conflict. None of this has in any way, had the same effect on me as when I began to read the diaries, journals, and letters of those who served in Battery B. Their stories moved me. They moved me enough to write this book.

My research for this book started by accident in the summer of 2019. I was on a family vacation when Phil DiMaria, the Captain of the modern-day living history group, First Rhode Island Battery B Light Artillery (a lifetime student of Battery B and longtime friend), sent me a couple of e-mails. I was intrigued.

These e-mails contained snippets of the diaries belonging to the soldiers in the Battery. At first, I was completely overwhelmed by the sheer volume, and in some cases, the scribbled and indecipherable writing. But, like a small trickle that slowly transforms into a deluge, I found that I could not read the material fast enough. I was mesmerized. After reading and studying hundreds of letters, diary entries, service records, and journals, I came to an interesting realization. After years of trying to get my family's interest in the Civil War by showing hundreds of bodies strewn across a battlefield, I realized that approach was not nearly as powerful as a photograph where a single soldier seemed to be staring back across the miles of history.

Through the exploration of Battery B's collection, I came to discover the story behind many of these soldiers. So many of these photos were fortunate enough to be accompanied by letters and diaries making for a much stronger connection between the individual and their experience. The more I read and reflected, the more I literally felt like I knew them. It was a strange feeling.

The mention of a family name, a mother or father, a brother or sister, a marriage certificate, a pension record, the names of their children, a lonely gravesite, all telling the story of their life before, during and, beyond the battles of the Civil War. I have come to understand now that this kind of personal account, this intimate connection, which untangles the knots and focuses on the individual, is the most powerful way to understand the true experience of those who lived during our nation's greatest conflict.

Like others, I have always found it difficult to grasp the concept of 650,000 casualties that the war inflicted. I could however begin to understand and empathize with one

Our Story

individual at a time. I could relate to his feelings and struggles. It all suddenly became real, very real.

I remember reading some of the soldiers' letters and somehow being transported back in time. I could see the expansive artillery camp, taste the hardtack, smell the mules, feel the cold rain, and hear their stories echo across the decades. For a moment, I felt like I was one of them, a Union cannoneer going through this strange and unsettling experience. I could feel the longing for family and the fear of not knowing whether one would ever return home. I experienced the sadness, the fatigue, the uncertainty, the pain, and the sacrifice.

It has changed the way I see the Civil War and how I think about it. It helped me to see that there is really no way to fully understand or deeply appreciate the Civil War purely from a collective perspective. It's just too big. At that level, it's all facts and grim statistics. To understand this struggle you need to strip away all the technical verbiage of corps, divisions, and brigades to appreciate these soldiers' experience at an individual level. You need to reach back in time and meet these individuals in their own space. When you get there, you will find that they are looking back at you, waiting for you to ask the question that they are longing to answer. What is your story?

Their stories are more than the story of the Civil War. Theirs, are the stories of longing, love, and loss. Their stories are not just facts. Their stories hold feelings often not found in history books. Their stories keep them alive and make them in some ways, immortal. It's only in asking this question that we can come to understand that these individuals were more than just soldiers. They were people just like us.

In April 1894, the remaining veterans of Battery B First Rhode Island Light Artillery published a regimental history chronicling their service during the Civil War. Thanks to the work of John H. Rhodes, the Battery's glorious service is explained in great detail beginning on August 13, 1861. It is a fascinating account of the Battery and it stands as a cornerstone to the historical significance of the Battery's role during the Civil War.

Given that this history already exists, the purpose of this book, in essence, is to present the reader with the unique experience of meeting these soldiers on a more personal level. This book is an attempt to bring to life a handful of the individuals who served in Battery B and present their stories so we can appreciate their humanity. In doing so, it is the hope of the author that readers will come to know these men not just as soldiers and heroes but as husbands, sons, fathers, nephews, friends, and brothers. This kind of biographical account of Battery B members to date has never been produced. It is, however, not exhaustive of every soldier who served in this unit. I wish it was but, to date, the information about Battery B and its members is still being discovered. The original historical material which has been preserved is thanks to Charles Tillinghast Straight who during the late 19th and early 20th century, made it his mission to preserve the Battery history in honor of his late father, Albert Aaron Straight, who served with Battery B.

Equal gratitude is owed to Phil DiMaria, who has spent a lifetime searching for, collecting and, preserving the original Battery artifacts, memoirs, records, journals, photos, and diaries. His dedication, commitment, and love for Battery B have made this book possible. I am indebted to Phil for sharing this historical material with me and am extremely grateful for his trust in me to write this book.

The aim of this book is to provide digestible but descriptive biographical sketches of the ordinary soldiers in Battery B whose stories long to be told. While the chapters are distinct from each other, together they tell of the Battery's legacy to the Union, which undoubtedly preserved the nation we know today.

The soldiers of Battery B were ordinary people who found themselves living during an extraordinary time. After all these decades, these individuals still find a way to shine through to us. When we look back, listen to their stories, read their letters and stare into their eyes, we discover who they really were. We also see something else that is truly astonishing. We see how similar they are to us. In some ways, their story is our story too.

Hot Work for Hazard's Battery, Walton Tabor, (Public Domain)

ALFRED GRAY GARDNER

1

"Tell My Wife I Died Happy"

On a hot July day in 1863, amidst the deafening roar of more than 200 artillery guns, Alfred Gray Gardner would spend the last few moments of his life dying in much the same way he lived, in prayer.

Forty-two years earlier in 1821, Alfred Gray Gardner was born on Christmas Day, the third son born to parents Job and Patience Gardner. He was born in an old house that had belonged to the Gardner family for many generations, called the Homestead, in Swansea, Massachusetts.

The Gardner Homestead by all accounts was a loving home, where the Gardner family held a deep Christian faith. As a boy, it was not uncommon for Alfred to see his home opened to strangers needing a place to stay for the night. Those who turned up at their door were never turned away. Instead, they were often provided a sense of hospitality and relief, whether in the form of food or drink or safety. Along with his brothers, he spent his childhood ice skating, fishing, and hunting. He loved nature and felt a sense of devotion to his family and his home.

As a student, he excelled at school, especially mathematics, and was known to others around him for his cheerful, gracious and, sincere demeanor. One winter, during his early teenage years, Alfred Gardner was stricken with a sudden illness that left him incapacitated for weeks. When he recovered, he emerged from his illness with a faith in God and a belief that all things were meant to be for his good. From that point forward, he maintained a sense of gratitude, even during trying times, owing his good fortune and life's blessings to God. At the age of 18, Gardner thought about becoming a surveyor but, his father Job, talked him out of it, asking for Alfred to stay and help on the family farm. Given his dedication to his parents and family, the young man agreed.

Six years later, the Reverend Israel Mashburn would marry 23-year-old Alfred and his 17-year-old bride, Adelia Wood, on a cold Monday afternoon, on February 3, 1845, in Somerset, Massachusetts. Two years later in 1847, they would have their first child, a daughter, Rosavele. In May 1850, their second daughter, Ida Mason Gardner was born. When Ida was just two years old, Alfred Gardner nearly died of another illness. This time he was sick for several months and doctors warned family members that he might not survive. Somehow, Alfred recovered and again emerged convinced that his return to health was due to God and those who were praying for him. In 1853, Gardner and his wife moved from Swansea to Fall River, Massachusetts. One year later, the Gardners would welcome their third child, Lillian, born May 11, 1854. Alfred and Adelia would have two more children, firstborn son, Alfred D.

Gardner on June 27, 1856, and their youngest Margaret (who they called Adelphia), born October 7, 1858. In all, Alfred and Adelia would have five children in thirteen years of marriage. Historical records show that Alfred Gardner moved from Fall River to Providence, Rhode Island sometime in the latter half of 1860. The family's decision to move across state lines was prompted by the need for a better education for his growing family and the prospects of a better life in Providence. The Census of 1860 shows that Alfred's personal estate was valued at an estimated $1,500 ($46,000 in 2020).

There is no doubt that Alfred Gardner was a dedicated father, husband and, family man. From his letters and diary entries, it is abundantly clear that he adored his family, loved his children and, had an unwavering devotion to his wife. That is why it was so difficult for Gardner to make the decision to enlist in the Union Army. He suffered through months of silent deliberation trying to balance the love of his family with the duty he felt to preserve the Union. Gardner finally made up his mind on August 8, 1862, when he appeared in a Union uniform telling his friends and family that he decided to 'do his duty'. From that moment on, Gardner would place his family and himself in the God he trusted so much.

Gardner would not enroll in Battery B originally but would instead enroll in Battery H First Rhode Island Light Artillery on the afternoon of Tuesday, August 12, 1862. A couple of weeks later his cousin, First Lieutenant John Gardner Hazard, who was assisting in the organization of Battery B, asked Alfred to transfer from Battery H to Battery B. Taking his cousin's advice, Alfred Gardner was mustered into federal service with Battery B on August 23, 1862.

In an extract from a letter to his cousin dated November 24, 1862, Gardiner explained his rationale for joining the Union Army. Again, his sense of faith and the strong conviction that God would provide for him and his family was quite evident.

He wrote the following: *"Dear Cousin, you say you were surprised to hear that I enlisted as a soldier. I will explain it. After the Battle of Bull Run, I felt it my duty to go and help but - my family - so dear to me! How could I leave them! I had no peace day or night until I decided. Since then, I have been a happy man. I have been in battle where balls and shells flew thick and fast, and no chance of dodging. I was on the field of Antietam for three days, and was cool and calm. I never felt the power of the Gospel as I did then. I did not enlist in a hurry, and when I left home, I left my family in the hands of God - I gave them to him, and I still hold the sacrifice dear to my heart. It not for me, now to trouble myself about my home. My object is to be prepared to meet my God at any time and this, I try to do as I go forth to do my duty. I told my family when I left them that I should not worry about them, I left them with one who would care for them. If they suffer on my account, I shall be very sorry, but I do not think they will. My country will not allow it. I do not think it is best for a man who has to face powder and ball to have much trouble with the things of this world. If I fall in battle, 'amen'. If I return to my family, again, 'amen'. Whatever is my duty, as I know it, that will I do with all my might, and the good Lord save us all in Heaven, where there will be no more, War."* In the roughly twelve months that Gardner would serve in Battery B, he would see and experience some of the biggest battles of the war, up close. Just a few days after leaving home he began writing letters to his family describing his experience in heartfelt accounts. One of his first letters home recounts his journey through Providence, Philadelphia, Baltimore, Washington, D.C. and finally Alexandria, Virginia.

Along the way, he was astounded by the way people received him, sometimes with applause. Some wanted to shake his hand. There is no doubt that he found it exciting, and he says as much in his letters. But his letters also show the strain and the early signs of the deprivation he would experience as a soldier. At one point he wrote to his wife saying, *"Had to sleep on the ground in an open field: stones a little troublesome at first till they got settled into the flesh."*

In late August 1862, Gardner found himself in Alexandria where the Second Battle of Bull Run had just been fought. He recounts seeing the dead being removed by the wagonload. He noted in his letters that, *"they looked sad enough."*

It's clear from his letters, specifically a letter dated August 30, 1862, that conditions and supplies were already a challenge for the Union Army. With no immediate possibility of getting rations, he wrote that for 37 cents, he was able to buy beefsteak, tomatoes, corn-cake, white bread and, *"good coffee"* from a house in Virginia that was apparently loyal to the Union. Though Gardner had his doubts, in that same letter home, he wrote the following:

"A very nice house only a few rods away where they keep a victualing table - call themselves "Union." I think they are imposters. Had a long talk with one of the ladies, the "Spy"; she has three brothers in the Army. Our troops were fired on from her house last summer and returned it with interest. The best well of water in Virginia is in her yard. Our troops guard her house, and we get water there for our canteens."

While Gardner clearly conveyed his thoughts about his less-than-ideal conditions, they were nothing compared to what the war had in store for him. By mid-September 1862, Gardner experienced first-hand the Battle of Antietam, wherein just one day, there would be more than 23,000 casualties. His account of that battle is poignant and no doubt was influenced by his faith and experiences growing up as a child on the Homestead. One of the greatest examples to serve both of these points comes in a letter he wrote one day after the battle. Not unlike the hospitality he witnessed at his boyhood home, Gardner's instinct toward cordiality and kindness are evident. He wrote to his wife that he shared his own limited supply of water with four *"full-blooded rebel"* prisoners who were very grateful for his generosity.

Antietam, September 18, 1862: "*All quiet now, but yesterday a terrible battle. Great losses on both sides. William and I are all right and ready for action at any moment and expect it. Haven't unhitched our horses for two days. Men and horses killed all around us. You would have heard something worth hearing if you had been here yesterday. The cannonading was terrific and continuous till dark. Found a good spring of water in the garden near the field. There is not a spot where you cannot see the dead and burying going on all the time. I have seen a battlefield. It is what I expected. I gave four prisoners water from my cup. They were full-blooded Rebels, but thanked me kindly. Battery B is here. Heavy firing. Wounded coming in by the car-loads. The religion of the Cross, I know by experience is everything. I found it good when the balls flew thick and fast around my head. It makes men brave in battle."*

Gardner's letters provide striking detail about the atmosphere after the battle at Antietam. He was still there three days later and recounts that the stench of the dead was nauseating. Bodies of dead horses and mules were piled high. A scene of death and destruction everywhere he looked. Despite the horror and bloodshed, Alfred would hear a band playing music for the injured soldiers in a field hospital as he walked through the rows of sick and wounded soldiers. Gardner was keenly aware of the significance of the moment he was living in. In his letters written from Antietam, he placed little pieces of stone in the envelope. Those stone fragments had been blown off a large boulder that had screened and protected him during the day's fight.

On September 20, 1862, he explained the experience in a letter to his cousin: *"I was on the battlefield of Antietam for three days. Men and horses lay in all directions and forms. I could count forty-five men so close to each other they were in heaps. Dead men whichever way you looked. Stayed on the field two nights. Was cool and calm. I never felt the honor of the Gospel as I did on that battlefield. I had no fear of death. Nothing like the religion of the Cross for a soldier. One thing was awful, the scent of the field; had to turn our back to it, and it was all we could do to keep our food down. Hundreds of men had lost all form of men. I have had a sight of all the scenes of a battlefield that be better imagined than described. I know what war means!"*

As the Army of the Potomac moved into the colder months of 1862, a rare winter battle took place at Fredericksburg, Virginia where Battery B was in the thick of the fight. Gardner describes the battle in somewhat poetic terms *"shells and mini-balls flew like raindrops in a gale."*

Gardner's service in Battery B would continue through the last months of 1862 and into the spring and summer of 1863. Like other soldiers, he came to appreciate treats and packages that were sent to the front from his family in Rhode Island. After six months in the rough fields and dense woods, Gardner received a package from his wife filled with pickled peaches, popcorn kernels, nuts, and dates. It's clear that the food invoked memories of home and a sense of longing for his family. In his response, he thanked his wife and added this endearing sentiment, *"Wouldn't mind seeing the children's little fingers in my plate this minute."*

Despite the suffering he experienced as a volunteer soldier Alfred Gardner seemed to keep a deep sense of peace about himself. In his spare time, he would go on *"tramp"* looking for rare flowers. He kept a small book with him where he would press flowers and then send them home to his wife. Throughout the many marches, he pointed out homes where huge gardens had been leveled by the advancing Union Army. At one point, he came across a home where a beautiful three-acre garden had been destroyed, *"fenceless and laid waste."* He witnessed former slave owners struggling to do work on their plantations where the slaves had fled; Union officers forcing Southern landowners to take the oath of allegiance while the women looked on in tears; army hospitals filled with the wounded; skulls and skeletons sticking out of the ground in places where hasty burial crews left the dead to rot; mud-soaked roads and; long campaigns carrying a 40-pound pack in the mid-day summer heat.

On June 29, 1863, Battery B marched thirty miles and camped eight miles outside of Gettysburg, Pennsylvania. According to Gardner, some of the strongest men were so tired they fell out of the ranks. Still, he pushed on with three days' worth of rations, his constant companion, his personal Bible, and his small book with pressed exotic flowers. When paper and stamps were scarce, Gardner wrote in the margins of his Bible. Here, he jotted down his thoughts of feeling cheerful even after a hard march and wishing his wife could hear the roar of the guns and be there for just a moment to experience what he felt. He noted thoughtfully, he would only have her come if there was a "*fast horse*" to whisk her home again. Such was the love he had for his wife.

And perhaps he was thinking of her when he was awoken at two o'clock on the morning on July 2, 1863, by the sound of bugles and officers' calls. The Battery was about to move into action. Gardner thought perhaps they might be getting attacked in the middle of the night but instead, realized they were to wait for orders to move. That morning, Alfred and his tent mates built a small fire, perked a pot of coffee and waited. As the sun came up, he was in motion on the Taneytown Road heading to Gettysburg. After a five-hour march, Battery B reached the field and went into the line of battle almost immediately.

Gardner saw hard fighting on July 2 as the Battery's position was badly exposed on the field. After firing dozens of rounds, the Battery was forced to pull back to a more secure position behind a stonewall on a ridge. That night, Gardner would pen some words in the margin of his Bible and fitfully sleep amidst the sound of wounded and dying men strewn in the field, just mere yards from where he would try to shut his eyes and rest. Perhaps he dreamt of home, Adelia, and his children. Perhaps he had nightmares of what he witnessed that day. Gardner awoke to a humid morning on July 3. No food. Hardly any water. He could hear distant fighting over the treetops as the Union and Confederate troops clashed on Culp's Hill. Then the morning and early afternoon became eerily quiet. Both armies were staring at each other over a mile-long open field. At one o'clock in the afternoon, a Confederate signal gun broke the silence. All at once, more than 100 Confederate cannons opened fire at the Union lines. Their guns trained on the Union center accentuated by a clump of trees. The Battery's fourth gun was positioned directly next to those trees and it's there that Alfred Gardner stood his post as the #2 man on his gun. For 15 minutes, Battery B soldiers waited to hear the command to fire, while the Confederate bombardment pummeled the federal line. Then Union commanders shouted orders and Gardner along with his comrades, Albert Straight, John Green, William Jones, John Delevan, and John Mowry went to work firing back at the rebel line. The cannons roared like thunder and smoke from the Union artillery now filled the field so profusely, it was hard to see the effect of their shots.

After more than an hour and a half of the Battery's constant firing, through the dense smoke, a rebel shell directly struck the mouth of the fourth gun at the exact moment that Alfred Gardner was ready to load a round of ammunition. As the shell smashed and exploded against the muzzle of the cannon, metal fragments tore into Gardner's left side, leaving his arm and shoulder hanging in shreds. Dazed, Gardner sat up against the wheel of the cannon, with a hole in his left side deep enough to expose his lung and other vital organs.

In shock and in pain, he had no idea that the same shell had also decapitated his friend, William Jones, whose dead body was now blown several yards forward. And so, it was. Alfred Gardner, the man who felt it was so important to serve, the man that others described as good, quiet, pious and always performing his duty, a man who tried to practice his belief, who stayed away from all the temptations of a soldier's life, was hemorrhaging from massive blood loss, his ribs and collarbone crushed to fragments. At that very same moment, Sergeant Straight saw what happened and sprinted to Alfred Gardner's side to fulfill and honor their mutual promise they both had made to each other when they enlisted months before. Sergeant Straight and Private Gardner had been tentmates and they pledged one another that if either one was ever killed or wounded, the survivor would come to the injured one's side. The day and moment they both dreaded, had finally arrived. Sgt. Albert Straight bent down on one knee and looked Gardner in the eyes. Sadly, Straight knew he was helpless to render any medical assistance or comfort. Laboring to take a full breath, Alfred Gardner asked his friend to please remove his treasured Bible and send it back home to his dear Adelia. *"Tell my wife, I died happy,"* he said as fatigue and disorientation began to set in. Mustering all the energy he had left, Gardner reached out with his right arm and shook the hand of his friend, Sgt. Albert Straight. Still grasping his hand, Gardner looked up at him and said goodbye.

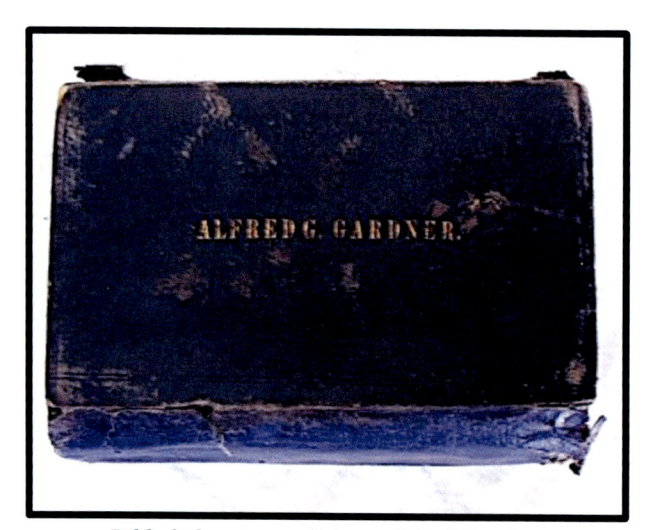

Bible belonging to Private Alfred Gardner

With narrowing vision, blood loss and, massive internal damage, Alfred spent the last two minutes of life, much in the same way he had spent the last 41 years, in prayer.

Gardner, who others often referred to as the 'Christian soldier' could be heard praying by those who witnessed his death even as the cannons thunderously roared around them. Gardner shouted, *"Glory to God, Halleluia. I am happy. Amen."* He took his last breath around 2:30 pm on the afternoon of July 3, 1863. At that same moment, with the Battery nearly out of men and ammunition, they were given the command to 'limber to the rear' and led off the field. It was at this time that Pickett's Charge commenced. Gardner's lifeless body would remain on the blood-soaked ground as 12,000 rebels advanced across the Emmitsburg Road and then were repulsed at the Union line atop Cemetery Ridge.

When the attack was over, Sergeant Straight took a group of men back to the Battery's position to retrieve supplies and equipment from the limber chests left after the battle. Sergeant Straight slowly approached Gardner's stiffened body and requested that another one of his Battery comrades, Sergeant Calvin Macomber, retrieve the tattered Bible

Cemetery Ridge Gettysburg, Pennsylvania

from Alfred's front pocket. Perhaps, Straight could not bring himself to do it. Perhaps, the trauma was still too fresh. Regardless, Macomber reached into Gardner's right pocket, took hold of the Bible and handed it to Sergeant Straight. The next morning, in the pouring rain, Sergeant Straight went back again to the same spot, this time with a larger detail of men to bury Gardner, Jones and, others who were left on the field overnight. The men buried Private Alfred Gardner almost exactly where he fell, together with his fallen comrade, William Jones. Straight wrapped them both in a red woolen blanket and buried them near a stone wall. He placed a wooden board at the head of the grave marked "*Alfred Gardner of Battery B First Rhode Island Lt. Artillery.*"

Thirteen days later, on July 16, 1863, Sergeant Straight wrote to Adelia Gardner telling her that her husband had been killed, that he died happily and, enclosed the Bible as requested. In the letter, he said that Gardner "*flinched not when the missiles of death flew thick about us*" and told the now widowed Adelia, where he had buried her husband. On July 28, 1863, Gardner's half-brother, John Gardner, arrived at Gettysburg and found his brother's body exactly where Straight had said he was buried. He took his brother's body out of the makeshift grave and spent the next eleven days carrying his lifeless half-brother back to Swansea, Massachusetts.

His body arrived at the Swansea Homestead on August 8, 1863, exactly a year to the day that Gardner arrived home in his new uniform proudly announcing he would enlist. That afternoon, Adelia and her five children, ages five to sixteen years old, placed him in a grave that he had dug himself, with his own hands, just days before he enlisted a year before in 1862. Adelia would receive an $8 monthly military pension for the rest of her life as a result of her husband's death. On August 23, 1863 (a year to the day that Alfred Gardner would leave Providence with the Battery) Adelia wrote to Sergeant Straight and thanked him for sending her Alfred's Bible. In her letter, she described the Bible as "*priceless.*" It's uncertain when or how it happened, but in the forty-four years after his death, Adelia would have inevitably opened Alfred Gardner's Bible and found the last words he would ever write. There, in the margin of his Bible, scribbled on July 2, 1863, were his final words, no doubt intended for his beloved wife and family to find after he was gone. It read: *"In Battery all ready for action. I am well in body and my mind is clear about the future. The prospect of Heaven has cheered me on this march from Falmouth to Pennsylvania. Children, be of good cheer, and always do right. This is the wish of your father."*

Cenotaph belonging to Alfred Gray Gardner, Gettysburg National Cemetery, Pennsylvania

Notes:
1. Alfred Gardner Biography, Brown University Library Collection
2. Massachusetts Census of 1860, Bristol, Massachusetts Ward 6 City of Fall River, July 11, 1860, M653, NARA Catalogue ID 2353568, Record Group 29 Records of the Bureau of the Census, National Archives, Washington, D.C.
3. Gardner, Alfred. Letter to his cousin. 24 November 1862. Brown University Library.
4. Gardner, Alfred. Letters to his wife Adelia Gardner. August 30 1862, September 18 1862, September 20 1862. Brown University Library Collection
5. John H. Rhodes, *The History of Battery B, First Regiment Rhode Island Light Artillery (Providence: Snow and Farnum, Printers, 1894)*, 209-211.
6. Gardner, Alfred. Letter to his wife Adelia. July 2 1862. Brown University Library Collection
7. Case Files of Approved Pension Applications of Widows and Other Veterans of the Army and Navy Who Served Mainly in the Civil War and the War with Spain, compiled 1861–1934, National Archives, Washington D. C. WC7995-Gardner-Alfred-G
8. Photo of Alfred Gardner is courtesy of the Swansea Historical Society
9. Photo of Alfred Gardner Bible is courtesy of the Varnum Armory Collection
10. Photo of Gettysburg Battlefield and grave of Alfred Gardner is courtesy of the Battery B First Rhode Island Light Artillery Inc. Collection.

JOHN GREENE

2

"Dead Range"

As the sun rose during the early morning hours of February 28, 1862, Battery B was encamped at the mansion of Alfred M. Barbour. Barbour, who had previously served as the Superintendent of the Harpers Ferry Armory, was serving as an officer in the Confederate army. With the mansion and other outlying structures deserted by Barbour and his wife Ella, the Battery's men occupied the large home, barn and, abandoned slave quarters. Greene would have first seen the Battery's guns neatly parked in the front yard as he came upon the scene for the first time as a new recruit. In the ensuing days, he and his new comrades would explore the town of Harpers Ferry, muse about its crumbling buildings, and visit the old engine house where two years earlier, Colonel Robert E. Lee captured John Brown.

Born in 1832, John Greene (who also used aliases of Brien, Breen, and Green) was the son of Daniel and Bridget O'Brien. He was born in the seaside village of Tully, Ireland. At some point before the age of 20, John immigrated to the United States and settled in Chicopee, Massachusetts. Like many millions of other Irish immigrants, it's possible he left Ireland to escape the potato famine and came to America looking for work and a better life. On February 17, 1852, John Greene married Johanna Connor, a young immigrant woman from Killarney, Ireland. Both being Roman Catholic, the two were married by Father William Blenkinsop at Saint Matthew's Church in Chicopee, Massachusetts.

After a couple of years of marriage, they had their first child, James, on July 7, 1854. In 1856, they had a daughter Bridget (named after John's mother) and, then a set of twin boys, John and Thomas who followed in September 1859. During these years, John worked as a laborer, most likely in Chicopee's mills. It is not clear exactly why, but by June 1860, John and Johanna were living in Brooklyn, New York. At the time, diseases and sickness were widespread in Chicopee and it is possible that John moved his family to escape the unsafe conditions.

John and Johanna would then move to Rhode Island sometime before the winter of 1862. Two days before the birth of their son, Daniel O'Brien, and just four days before their tenth wedding anniversary, John Greene said goodbye to his wife and children and joined the Union cause with Battery B on February 13, 1862.

Described as a *"sturdy Irishman,"* John saw immediate action at the battle of Fair Oaks, Seven Pines, and Savage's Station during the spring of 1862. On December 4, 1862, John wrote to his wife Johanna, saying he was glad to have received her letter and promised to send money home soon. He would have had no idea of the horrific fighting that awaited him just nine days later at the first battle at Fredericksburg. At around 3:45 in the afternoon of December 13, 1862, Battery B proceeded on the double-quick and galloped into position just a short-range from the Confederate's nearly impregnable position. So dangerous and precarious was Battery B's position on the field that nearby Battery A soldiers saluted them with, *"There goes Battery B to hell."* For three-quarters of an hour, John Greene and the men of Battery B would suffer under horrendous fire. The thud of mini balls hitting flesh and the groans of wounded men filled the smoky air. Fortunately for Greene, he was not counted among the Battery's sixteen wounded by the day's end.

On July 1, 1862, Battery B was engaged with a Confederate force at Malvern Hill. Rebel artillery shells were finding their targets; many of them exploding directly in front of Battery B's position. With lightning speed and horrific sound, shells were striking the ground and then bouncing through the Battery's gun carriages taking out whatever was in their path. One exploding shell fragment broke a horse's leg off while another struck an artillerist in the forehead. Despite the danger, John Greene remained at his post servicing the Battery's guns. As the morning fighting progressed, a shell fragment struck Greene in the arm, though he was not badly wounded. But as the afternoon wore on, the firing became more intense. At one point, an airburst shell exploded overhead. As it rained down shrapnel, another shell fragment hit Greene in the leg. Rather than being scared, Greene was angry. He jumped up and down and cursed the enemy. *"The damn rebels has got the dead range on me sure."* The wounded Greene would recover from his injuries but the men would jokingly remind him of the incident afterward saying, *"Look out John, the rebels has got a dead range on you"*, an eerie prediction that would, unfortunately, come to pass.

Greene would write home again on February 8, 1863. Just a couple of days before, a blanket of snow covered the ground and the men suffered one of the coldest winters ever experienced in Falmouth, Virginia. In his letter, he wishes his wife would write more often and wonders if she is receiving the money he sent home. The tone of the letter is a bit worrisome and he is clearly concerned about the mundane details of home life. In the postscript, John asks his wife to see if they can stay in the home where they are living for another year. He writes:

"My pen in hand to let you know that I am well and hope to find you enjoying the same blessing. I have wrote four letters and got no answer. I sent a check for ten dollars. I would like to know whether you received it or not. I made inquiry about Bill Nooman and could hear anything about him. The ninth and sixth army is moving and we don't know how soon we will move. I wish you would be more prompt about writing to me. Write as soon as possible and let me know how you are getting along. Let me know if you are getting anything from the town or not. Direct to Battery B RI. Gen. Sumner Right Grand Division, Washington, DC. No more at present from most loving husband. John Greene

If I don't get home by April, find out whether you can have the place or not for another year.

John would not return home by April 1863. Instead, after several months in camp, John Greene was on the march back to Fredericksburg for yet another murderous battle. Surviving another deadly engagement, John Greene and Battery B would find themselves in June 1863, following the Army of Virginia into Pennsylvania. On July 1, the two great armies collided at Gettysburg. On July 3, 1863, after two days of deadly fighting, John Greene remained at his post on the gun. As the number four man on the Battery's fourth gun commanded by Sergeant Straight, he would have been using all of his strength to pull the lanyard that would fire the cannon. Hungry and tired, John Greene had not eaten in two days as the Battery's ration wagon arrived late, and the cannoneers had already been called to their posts.

Once again, Battery B held a critical spot on the field. Battery B's position near the copse of trees on Cemetery Hill was in the direct center of Lee's final assault. Over the course of an hour and a half, John Greene performed his duty firing dozens of rounds at the enemy's lines. Then at around 2:30 in the afternoon, in the blazing heat, a rebel shell struck the muzzle of the fourth gun. As it exploded, hot metal fragments struck the Battery's crew. Alfred Gardner, the gun's number two-man, had his left arm and shoulder nearly torn off. William Jones, the gun's number one man, decapitated. Standing just three feet away from both Gardner and Jones, Greene felt the powerful blast wave and was hit by flying body parts and brain matter. Wiping away the blood from his eyes, Greene witnessed Sergeant Straight kneel down to hear Gardner's last dying words. Then Sergeant Straight rose up and turned toward the gun. He tried to force a solid round down the barrel in an attempt to fire the piece again but the muzzle of the gun was dented from the explosion.

Greene heard Lieutenant Charles A. Brown call for an axe to be brought up from caisson so Sergeant Straight could ram the round down the barrel of the gun. As Sergeant Straight whaled on the round with an axe, another rebel shell struck the cannon. As the shell exploded, several pieces of shrapnel penetrated Greene's exhausted body. Wounded, Greene slumped to the ground and would remain on the field in his blood-soaked uniform until late in the afternoon when Sergeant Straight returned and removed Private Greene to a triage station behind Union lines. Greene languished for thirteen days in the heat and aftermath of the battle. He expired at a temporary field hospital in Gettysburg on July 16, 1863.

Battery B officially recorded his death on the rolls on August 12, 1864, but Johanna no doubt received the grim news of her husband's death months earlier. She began filing for widow's benefits in April 1864. With five young children, Johanna would have needed this income to support her family. The pension records reveal that she went through quite an ordeal trying to prove just who her husband was owing to the fact that he used different last names at different times throughout his life and service during the war. Born John O'Brien, he used Breen, Brien, and Greene interchangeably. From her home in Hopkinton, Rhode Island, Johanna would enlist neighbors in Westerly and former employers to attest that John Greene was also Breen and Brien. Eventually, she proved her case and would receive $8 a month in widows' benefits and $2 each month for each of her five children. Johanna would never remarry and died at the age of 82 on April 4, 1914. John Greene's body is interred at the Gettysburg National Cemetery in Gettysburg, Pennsylvania, in the Rhode Island Section. He was 31 years old at the time of his death.

John Greene Letter dated February 8, 1863 to his wife Johanna

John Greene Grave at Gettysburg

Notes:
1. Case Files of Approved Pension Applications of Widows and Other Veterans of the Army and Navy Who Served Mainly in the Civil War and the War With Spain, compiled 1861 - 1934 **Brien, John S (WC55132)**.
2. NARA M653. Eighth Census of the United States, 1860 population schedules.
3. John H. Rhodes, *The History of Battery B, First Regiment Rhode Island Light Artillery (Providence: Snow and Farnum, Printers, 1894),* 61, 101-102, 139, 209-214.
4. Delevan, John. Presentation at Gettysburg. July 2&3 1863. Battery B First Rhode Island Light Artillery Inc. Collection.
5. Skipmunk, The Story of Chicopee: *http://www.chicopeepubliclibrary.org/archives/files/original/6c8b06681ef2a3e3907202567e9669e3.pdf,* 24-25, 29.
6. Plourde-Barker, Michele, *Chicopee* (Arcadia Publishing, 1998), 116.
7. Photo of Greene courtesy of Battery B First Rhode Island Light Artillery Inc. Collection
8. Photo of John Green Grave courtesy of Battery B First Rhode Island Light Artillery Inc. Collection

SAMUEL J. GOLDSMITH

3

"They Will Find Heroes Here"

Thirty-eight-year-old Corporal Samuel Goldsmith fought as a Union artillerist with Battery B First Rhode Island Light Artillery at Gettysburg on July 2-3, 1863. A couple of weeks after the battle, Goldsmith was in camp in Pleasant Valley, Maryland, and wrote home to his wife Sarah in Rhode Island. Taking shelter in his tent from the driving summer rain, Goldsmith penned one of the most heartfelt and celebrated letters of the Battery B collection. The letter was completed over a two-day-period starting the morning of July 17th in Maryland and was finished the evening of July 18th in Virginia at sunset. It is a window into the relationship between newly married Samuel and Sarah Goldsmith.

His letter with powerful diction and alliteration *("reptile rebellion"* and *"cowardly curses")* expresses a wide spectrum of emotion. His thoughts address everything from suffering to humor to courage, to duty and, to love. Goldsmith's poignant and eloquent words profess a profound passion of sentiment towards his wife and his family. While the letter touches many subjects from the concern of his elderly father to the fact that he has been unable to wash his clothes, the letter is, above all, an enduring love letter. Goldsmith reveals in vivid terms, his love for Sarah, his pride in the Battery, his duty towards his country, and his ultimate faith in God.

The language is beautiful and at times hauntingly sad. *"My Darling good Wife,"* the letter begins, *"I am happy to inform you that I am well and hope you and all my family and friends are the same."* As the letter unfolds, Goldsmith tries to somehow convey the enormous suffering he has endured. Failing to find the adequate words or where to start he shares his sense of loss in tangible terms, *"I have lost all my things twice and I have nothing now except what is on my body. But the loss that grieves me the most is two little pictures, my wife and my poor little girls."*

His letter goes on to tell his wife of the bravery of the men he is fighting with and says, *"None of the Rhode Island sons turned their backs to the enemy, they stood to their posts like good men they are."*

Throughout the letter, Goldsmith professes his deep love for his wife, *"If I were home now,"* he writes, *"I would kiss my gallant little wife."* In fact, three times throughout the letter, Goldsmith wishes he could give his wife a kiss. In one of the most enduring lines of the letter, Goldsmith tells his wife that he just had a *"good pot of coffee"* but would rather be drinking tea with her. His deep love for his wife is also felt in what he doesn't write. He knows the details of the battle at Gettysburg would be too frightening to share and therefore, tries to shield her from her own imagination. *"I will not try to tell you anything about it for I cannot if I try, your fancy will paint the horrible sights better than I can describe them."*

The letter also echoes his love for his children. As the sun goes down and the daylight begins to fade, he writes, *"Now Darling I must kiss you goodnight, kiss my babes for me."* He also expresses his belief and trust in God, *"I hope He will protect me and send me home to help you with your hard lot."* Like other soldiers during the war, his words carry the weight of an unknown future and fate.

Sarah, 22-years old, would have received the letter a couple of weeks later in early August. She would have not known at the time that Samuel Goldsmith would be eventually captured and taken prisoner on August 25, 1864, at Ream's Station, Virginia. He would remain a prisoner for four months and in due course be released on November 26, 1864. He would be reunited with Battery B and formally discharged on May 26, 1865. When the war ended, he returned to Rhode Island and his family. Samuel Goldsmith lived to be 92 years old. He died in 1917. He and his wife Sarah and their daughter, Ester, are buried at Spears Cemetery in Foster, Rhode Island.

The letter that follows below has been transcribed for simplicity and ease of reading. Where necessary, phonetic spelling has been corrected and punctuation added for ease of reading. Despite these small editorial changes, the Goldsmith letter remains a touchstone in Battery B correspondence. His words, poetic, thoughtful, and ultimately hopeful, still reach across the centuries and touch us as they did in 1863.

Pleasant Valley Maryland near Harpers Ferry Va. Friday, July 17, 1863

"My Darling good Wife I am happy to inform you that I am well and hope you and all of my family and friends are the same. I do not know how to write to you today. I have so much to tell you that I do not know what to write first. I have seen and suffered much since we left Falmouth. I have lost all of my things twice and I have nothing now except what is on my body.

But the loss that grieves me most is two little pictures my wife and my poor little girls. Now I see, in case you want to know how lost them, it is a long tale to tell. If you was sitting by my side this rainy morning I would tell you lots of news some that would make you laugh but more of a different nature, more cry than laugh. I will tell you that we have some great stalwart fellows in this Battery that are always boasting of their courage of what they have done, of what they would do. But when the reb comes, when the time arrives for the man to show himself, these boasting heroes run off like some stinking sons of b……s. That is a hard name to give anything but it is impossible for an honorable woman to bring out such sneaking cowardly curses. But I am glad to tell you that none of Rhode Island sons turned their backs to the enemy, they stood to their posts like good men as they are. But some of our larger states that boast sending so many men to the field have did least good. There is one state that has sent 140 regiments of infantry to the war that are not worth so much as ten such regiments as the 15 Mass. But I must not criticize closely. The 15, 19, 20, and 4th RI are not to be whipped by a force of twice their numbers. The battle of the 2nd and 3rd July were the hardest ever fought in the new world. I doubt if Europe ever saw the like. Napoleon fought some great battles but Meade has fought a greater. I will not try to tell anything about it for I cannot. If I try, your fancy will paint the horrible sights better than I can describe them. I can only tell you my love that on the 3rd the rebs opened fire on us with 104 cannons against 36 of ours. Their artillery formed a half circle. Ours was a straight line like this. The B shows the position of our battery. Now is it any wonder that our Battery was drove to pieces and that we have no guns. We are with Battery A now but we shall have a set of guns soon. Well, my love I cannot write anymore now. I will write more tomorrow."

Saturday, July the 18, 1863

"Well Sarah what do you think now. Here we are away out in Virginia. I thought we should stop in Maryland long enough to rest and wash our clothes for we are as dirty as hogs. But such is not the case. We are in camp now one good long day's march from Harpers Ferry. I don't know what Gen. Meade is up to but I think he is making for the South Bank of the Rappahannock. If so, you may look out for some more tall fighting.

I hear good news from our boys down South. If the reports are true the rebs are about played out. And the 300,000 drafted men will wind up their crazy old clock so tight for them that they will die for want of time. I see by the papers that John and Bert Greaves are drafted, also old man Martin. I hope they will prove good men true. 300,000 hearts of oak at this time will crush the vile reptile rebellion to death in a short time. Tell the boys to come. They will find heroes here to lead them on and heroes to back them up. If I was home now I would kiss my gallant wife, *guard my armor and away to the field strife and slaughter. I know that no man is fit to have a Country who will not defend it from insult with his blood if called. No.*

Well, my little wife I must kiss you and our darlings good night for the sun is most down and cannot get candles on the march so I have but a short time to write. I have just had a good pot of coffee but I should like to have a cup of tea with you tonight. My darling noble wife I am sorry that you should think I was finding fault with you on account of my poor old Father. I know love that your great good heart would be willing to do all that you can for him. You always have done all that you could for him. I do not ask you to take him to live with you. Do what you think to be your duty and God will bless you and I hope he will protect me and send me home to help you with your hard lot. Now darling I must kiss you goodnight. Kiss my babes for me. Give my love to all of our friends and may God bless you for your goodness. Write to my Cousin and to me. Good night."

Your husband, Samuel Goldsmith
To his wife Sarah J. Goldsmith

Grave site of Samuel J. Goldsmith, his wife and his daughter, Spears Cemetery Foster, Rhode Island

Notes:
1. John H. Rhodes, *The History of Battery B, First Regiment Rhode Island Light Artillery* (Providence: Snow and Farnum, Printers, 1894) 226
2. Goldsmith, Samuel J. Letter to his wife. 17 July 1863, 18 July 1863. Courtesy of Fred Piza Private Goldsmith Collection
3. *Find a Grave*, database and images (https://www.findagrave.com: accessed 24 October 2020), memorial page for Samuel J. Goldsmith (1825–1917), Find a Grave Memorial no. 59581239, citing Spears Cemetery, Foster, Providence County, Rhode Island, USA; Maintained by Nate Bramlett (contributor 46874243).
4. Photo of Samuel Goldsmith courtesy of Battery B First Rhode Island Light Artillery Inc. Collection

DAVID BURLINGAME KING

4

"Limber to the Rear"

David Burlingame King was born in 1836, the son of Abin and Phebe King, in Cranston, Rhode Island. On August 13, 1861, he was one of the original 139 men who enlisted in Battery B at the armory of the Providence Marine Corps of Artillery on Benefit Street in Providence, Rhode Island. Not much is known about why King decided to enlist but, in so doing, he left behind his eighteen-year-old wife, Mary King, to tend to their home in Scituate, Rhode Island. They were both likely unaware at the time that Mary was pregnant.

At 4:00 on the afternoon of March 27, 1862, King was on the move marching down Pennsylvania Avenue destined for Georgetown where he would embark on a transport ship to Alexandria, Virginia. That day, Mary gave birth to their son. She named him after his father, David Herbert King.

During the sweltering afternoon of July 2, 1863, as the battle of Gettysburg intensified, the six guns of Battery B were positioned on Cemetery Ridge close to the Codori Farm. As King and his fellow artillerists fired shot after shot across the Emmitsburg Road, they saw hundreds of men emerge from the woods on their left. At first, they thought they were Union troops. They realized their mistake when they heard the distinctive rebel yell of General Ambrose Wright's Georgia Brigade. Exposed and under concentrated fire, Battery B fired double canister rounds at point-blank range at the advancing enemy.

Amidst the confusion, the Battery was ordered to 'limber to the rear' and began moving their six guns off the field. They struggled to move the six 12-pound Napoleons back through a narrow opening in a stone wall and seek cover behind the Union lines. As they all tried to press through this gap, confederate infantry aimed at the helpless horses. Within minutes, every horse was killed and the gun crews were forced to abandon some of their guns and seek protection behind the wall. That is, all but the gun crew of the Battery's fourth gun.

Even though ordered to 'limber to the rear', Sergeant Straight and the crew remained in their position, determined to fire one additional round of ammunition. Helping to fire that round was David King. Once fired, the men were ordered to look out for themselves and take cover wherever they could. Confederate soldiers overtook the Battery's position. One Confederate took aim and fired a shot at David King. He fell to the ground and lived just a few minutes. Sergeant Straight's diary entry dated July 2, 1863 memorializes this moment:

"We were ordered to limber to the rear when they (the rebs) had got very near to us, two of my horses were shot just as the order was given, and I could not get

my piece off, and the boys had to look out for themselves, as the Johnnies were all around us, and the bullets flew very lively, with some shot and shell, all my horses were killed. David B. King was hit and lived but a few minutes and one man was taken prisoner. I got my piece off again after the charge was over." King's body would remain on the field through the afternoon and night of July 2nd and all day and night of July 3rd as the battle culminated with Pickett's Charge. On July 4, 1863, Sergeant Straight and a small detachment of men, buried King's body near a stone wall along with cannoneers Alfred G. Gardner and William Jones.

Four months after the battle, King's body was moved to the Gettysburg National Cemetery. Mary King would eventually file for widow's benefits in the name of her fallen husband who would never meet his son. King also has a cenotaph at the Smithville Cemetery in Scituate, Rhode Island.

Death Certificate of David B. King

David B. King grave marker in the Rhode Island Section at Gettysburg National Cemetery, Pennsylvania

David B. King cenotaph at Smithville Cemetery, Rhode Island

Notes:
1. John H. Rhodes, *The History of Battery B, First Regiment Rhode Island Light Artillery (Providence: Snow and Farnum, Printers, 1894), 202-204*
2. Pension Certificate of Mary King, Fold3, The National Archives, King, D B (WC20078), NARA Catalogue ID 30020
3. Photo of David B. King courtesy of Battery B First Rhode Island Light Artillery Inc. Collection
4. *Find a Grave*, database and images (https://www.findagrave.com: accessed 25 October 2020), memorial page for David B. King (1836–1863), Find a Grave Memorial no. 114848109, citing Smithville Cemetery, North Scituate, Providence County, Rhode Island, USA; Maintained by Beth Hurd (contributor 48126691)

DAVID B. PATTERSON

5

The Retreat

Both legs remained broken. Almost eleven weeks after a one-ton gun carriage ran over both of his legs at Savage's Station, David Patterson was confined to his bed on a cool fall afternoon in Chester, Pennsylvania. Initially, his injuries had gone unattended and now Patterson was suffering from the extreme pain of multiple broken bones.

Patterson enlisted in Battery B as a corporal when the Battery was formed on August 13, 1861. He was an able and youthful man, who by all accounts, was promoted early on for being a skilled and intelligent soldier. But just a year into his military service, his young body was shattered.

Patterson had seen the terrors and horrors of war since he volunteered. He was at Ball's Bluff where men were forced to escape by jumping into the Potomac River; some with musket balls still lodged in their extremities. Many soldiers drowned. Others were never seen or heard from again. The danger was omnipresent and every day presented another chance for injury or death.

For Patterson, his luck ran out on June 29, 1862. It was a Sunday, day 5 of the 7 Days-Battle of Savage's Station, Virginia, and the Battery had been on the move all day, marching toward the line of battle. Throughout the day the sound of cannon fire and muskets echoed from the front lines. It was six o'clock in the evening when Patterson and the six-gun crews of Battery B reached the reserve line of the battle. In the growing dusk, Patterson could see the famous Irish Brigade as they prepared to enter the woods and face an imminent Confederate attack. Men on horseback were galloping along the lines to the cheers and shouts of the infantry, who tried to get their courage up. A few incoming artillery shells had already passed close to Battery B and the cannoneers were forced to move to safety in a hurry.

The men leaped onto anything they could to avoid the inbound projectiles. Some artillerists jumped onto the gun trails while others hung tightly to the limbers as they pulled their guns to a more protected position. As the gun detachments wheeled out hastily onto Williamsburg Road, they quickly realized they were not alone. Other batteries and wagons were also lurching down the congested road filling it with a morass of limbers, caissons and, battery wagons. With all the human and animal traffic clogging the escape route, the Battery's gun crews pulled off the road into a cornfield, hoping to gain speed and bypass the congested mass of mules and men blocking the egress route. Patterson and two other soldiers, Joseph Luther and Allen Burt clung on for their dear life as they sat locking arms atop the sixth gun's limber chest. As they bounced and pitched their way through the corn stubble, one of the limber wheels plunged into a hole, throwing Patterson, Luther and, Allen off the chest. Allen and Luther hit the ground hard but were able to roll out of harm's way. Patterson wasn't so fortunate. As he fell into the trampled cornstalks, the gun carriage, weighing roughly 2,000 pounds ran him over. As it diagonally crossed over him, the wheel first crushed his left thigh and then rolled over several bones in his right ankle as it trailed away.

Dazed and in shock, Patterson could hear the officers' orders to keep moving forward. The situation was chaotic, and little time could be afforded to wait or stop. Out of the corner of his eye, Patterson saw Allen and Luther unhurt, climb back on the limber. Instinctually, he tried to do the same but was unable to feel his legs.

A couple of cannoneers saw him on the ground and jumped off to tend to him. They carried him out of the way of the moving tangle of trains and wagons, laid him against a tree, then ran to catch up to the moving limber that was already several yards away. In the growing darkness, Patterson was alone but not for long. Within minutes, the Confederate infantry swamped the position and took Patterson, prisoner.

For exactly a month, Patterson languished in a Richmond prison. Despite his horrific wounds, Confederate doctors did not provide medical treatment. On July 29, 1862, after thirty days as a prisoner of war, Confederate soldiers loaded Patterson onto a railcar on route to City Point, Virginia. The ride was a living nightmare. Unable to properly steady himself, Patterson endured the inhumane 23-mile torture, as his weak body bounced and pounded against the floor and walls of the car. Any healing that might have taken place during his captivity was in vain. As the train cars pitched and jostled making their way south toward the James River, Patterson's legs broke again.

At City Point, Virginia, Patterson, nauseated and emaciated, found himself part of a prisoner exchange. Once transferred over to the Federal Army, it would take another sixteen days before he finally arrived at a Union field hospital outside of Chester, Pennsylvania. There, Union doctors would finally go about the task of setting his legs. They did the best they could but his right ankle would never set exactly straight. His left leg would not fare much better. More than a month after being crushed, his left leg was three inches shorter than his right one. Doctors would attempt to stretch his leg by strapping it to the bed and attaching a sandbag to pull it down as far as possible.

Eventually alerted by a letter home, Patterson's mother would travel from Worcester, Massachusetts to Pennsylvania to briefly be with her son. She would return north and tell the family of her son's tragic accident.

Still, throughout his ordeal, Patterson tried to remain cheerful and optimistic. On the 30-day anniversary of his arrival to the Union hospital he wrote to his sister Margaret: *"I may think myself lucky towards some men here, with their legs off. I am getting along nicely now since I came here. I have the best of care taken of me and all it needs now is time and patience."* Even though Patterson could not sit upright for more than eleven weeks, he made it a point to write letters home to his sister Margaret and brothers, Horatio and Andrew. But, in addition to the physical pain he endured, Patterson also suffered the emotional pain inflicted by his brother, John. Despite writing six letters to his brother since his enlistment in 1861, John never wrote one letter back. On January 10, 1863, Patterson, still confined to his bed, implored his brother once more to write back saying, *"I am anxious to hear from you."* He accused him of being *"careless of writing"* but, eventually concludes his letter with, *"I remain your loving brother."*

Patterson would linger in the hospital throughout February 1863. He eventually regained the use of his legs and walked with the support of a cane. He would be formally discharged from Battery B on March 25, 1863. David Patterson would go on to live the rest of his life in Worcester, Massachusetts. He is buried at Mount Saint Mary's Cemetery in Pawtucket, Rhode Island.

Notes:
1. John H. Rhodes, *The History of Battery B, First Regiment Rhode Island Light Artillery* (Providence: Snow and Farnum, Printers, 1894), 96-98
2. Patterson, David. Letter to his family. 15 September 1862, 10 January 1863, Courtesy of Battery B First Rhode Island Light Artillery Inc. Collection
3. Photo of David Patterson is courtesy of Battery B First Rhode Island Light Artillery Inc. Collection

AMOS HORTON ARMINGTON

6

A Life of Service

At 1:00 on the afternoon of May 6, 1924, the small borough of Danielson, Connecticut fell eerily silent. Storekeepers and shop owners shut their doors during the middle of the day out of respect for the man who pallbearers were carrying up the narrow aisle that led to the church altar.

The bells in the bell tower tolled as state and town officials, members of the Women's Relief Corps, and dozens of mourners filled the pews of Saint Alban's Episcopal Church where one of Danielson's most respected and beloved citizens was being laid to rest. When the hallowed service started, Reverend Leonard Richards asked the congregation to pray for the deceased, Amos Horton Armington. Seventy-eight years earlier, Armington was born on August 19, 1845, in Seekonk, Massachusetts (now a part of East Providence, Rhode Island). He was one of four children and received an education in both private and public schools in the area. At age 17, Armington enlisted in Battery A First Rhode Island Light Artillery on May 22, 1862. Though only a young private, Armington would experience some of the fiercest battles of the Civil War. After nearly four months to the day he enlisted, Amos would find himself posted on a small hill near the Hagerstown Pike at the Battle of Antietam near Sharpsburg, Maryland on the humid morning of Wednesday, September 17th, 1862. On that deadly day, where there were more than 23,000 casualties, Armington would serve on one of Battery A's six artillery pieces. In four hours, Battery A fired more than 1,000 rounds at the advancing Confederate infantry and opposing Confederate artillery forces. When Battery A was finally relieved, they would add to the casualty count with four dead and 15 men wounded. Armington would not be one of them. He would survive that battle only to find himself again locked in another deadly fight in the countryside of Pennsylvania a year later. Armington fought on the contested ground of Cemetery Ridge at Gettysburg. There along with Battery A cannoneers, Armington would experience the gruesome reality of war as

Saint Albans Episcopal Church (courtesy of the Episcopal Church of Connecticut)

Confederate artillery shells and projectiles exploded incessantly around the Battery's critical position. Armington likely witnessed the tragic deaths of his comrades who fought bravely at their posts. Comrades like John Zimla who would be decapitated by an exploding shell; John Higgins who would have his arm and shoulder blown off; and Patrick Lannegan who would be shot in the stomach. Months later, their bodies would be buried in the Rhode Island section of the Gettysburg National Soldiers Cemetery. But Armington would live to see more combat in the Battle of the Wilderness and Petersburg.

On September 23, 1864, Battery A First Rhode Island Light Artillery was officially consolidated with Battery B First Rhode Island Light Artillery. On that day, Sergeant Armington joined Battery B and would remain with the Battery until the war's end in April 1865. **On May 21, 1865,** Armington was formally mustered out of the Battery and returned home to Rhode Island. There, five years later, Amos would marry Susan Allen White Armington on May 18, 1870. Together they would have one child, Frederic Armington, on August 3, 1872. In 1878, Armington and his family would move to Danielson, Connecticut, where he would open a fruit and ice cream business. Ten years later, along with his son, Armington would open his own grocery store in 1888.

As a civilian and successful merchant, Armington dedicated himself to a life of public service. He was a member of the Court of Burgesses in the borough of Danielson for six years. During that time, he would make significant improvements to the roads, gardens, and parks of the small town. He served two terms in the Connecticut House of Representatives, served as warden of Saint Alban's Church and quartermaster of the Grand Army of the Republic. On April 10, 1905, he became warden of the Borough of Connecticut and on August 12, 1922, he was elected President of the Battery B Veteran Association by his surviving comrades. Perhaps the call to public service was in his blood as Armington's great-great-great-great-grandfather, Joseph Jencks, served as Governor of Rhode Island from 1727-1732.

In late April 1924, Amos Armington began to fall ill with a bladder infection. His health continued to deteriorate for two weeks until on Sunday, May 4th, at 1:15 in the afternoon, when he passed away at his home. Two days later, on Tuesday, May 6th, the choir at Saint Alban's would sing a final hymn to the fallen soldier and esteemed citizen. They sang the hymn *"Lead, Kindly Light"* whose heartfelt lyrics no doubt, described the young private's feelings as a teenager on the front lines, *"The night is long and I am far from home."* Perhaps Reverend Richards recounted Amos's extraordinary achievements and his three long years at war where Armington never missed a day of service to either disease or wounds and was recorded on the rolls as the youngest member of Battery A.

Armington was buried a day later on May 7, 1924, in the Westfield Cemetery in Danielson, Connecticut, where he and his wife lie in repose today.

Headstone of Amos and Susan Armington, Westfield Cemetery, Connecticut

Notes:
1. John H. Rhodes, *The History of Battery B, First Regiment Rhode Island Light Artillery* (Providence: Snow and Farnum, Printers, 1894), 335
2. William Harrison Taylor, *Taylor's Legislative History and Souvenir of Connecticut, 190-: Portraits and Sketches of State Officials, Senators, Representatives, Etc. List of Committees. Portraits and Roll of Delegates to Constitutional Convention of 1902. The Proposed Constitution and the Vote, Volume 5* (Putnam Connecticut, William Harrison Taylor, 1905-1906)
3. https://civilwarintheeast.com/us-regiments-batteries/rhode-island/rhode-island-battery-a/
4. Photo of Armington courtesy of Battery B First Rhode Island Light Artillery Inc. Collection
5. Photo of Saint Albans Church courtesy of the Episcopal Church of Connecticut
6. *Find a Grave,* database and images (https://www.findsagrave.com: accessed 24 October 2020), memorial page for Amos Horton Armington (19 Aug 1845-4 May 1924), Find a Grave Memorial no. 43594579, citing Westfield Cemetery, Danielson, Windham County, Connecticut, USA; Photo by Nate Bramlett.

WILLIAM DENNIS

7

The Wilderness

William Dennis slowly sipped on a cup of steaming hot coffee. It was his first warm drink in many days. The forage wagons had finally arrived the night before and provided much-needed supplies to his unit's dwindling provisions. Conditions over the last few days in early May 1864 had been rough. Dennis, a cannoneer of Battery B, was engaged in the Battle of the Wilderness. The fighting over deep ravines and steep ridges made the movement of the artillery guns very difficult. For the moment though, in the quiet early morning hours of May 9, 1864, William savored a small piece of salt pork and soaked his hardtack in his coffee for breakfast. As he ate, he could hear the horses nearby being groomed and finally fed after days of brutally exhausting work. The morning lull, however, would not last long. Captain Fred Brown ordered the men to hitch the horses and be ready to move again. Battery B was heading back to the front.

William Dennis was twenty years old when he enlisted in Battery B on August 13, 1862. He was born in Ireland in 1842 to parents Jemmey and Catherine (Gorman) Dennis. His father died when William was only four years old and it's likely that the widowed mother and son immigrated to the United States shortly after his death. By 1860, they were renting a tenement house on 18 Acorn Street in Providence, Rhode Island. William paid the rent from the earnings he made as an apprentice jeweler before the war and supported his mother during his enlistment, sending his military wages home.

In February 1864, just three months before the Wilderness Campaign, William had been part of a group of veteran volunteers who were granted a thirty-five-day furlough for having re-enlisted in Battery B near Stevensburg, Virginia. That commitment to re-enlist in the Battery would allow William to go home and see his mother for the first time in almost two years. And it would be the last time Catherine would see her son.

On the afternoon of May 9, 1864, William and the gun detachments of Battery B were positioned along the Po River in Virginia. Across the water, a Confederate wagon train was winding its way along a dirt road. In the afternoon heat, Lieutenant Gideon Spencer's gun crew, which included William Dennis, fired several spherical case shells over the river in the direction of the enemy. But before long, the Confederate batteries returned their fire and began to open up on Battery B's position on the river bank. A shell from one of those batteries burst and struck Dennis and another soldier killing them instantly. The news of her son's death traveled quickly to Providence. Three weeks later on May 31, 1864, destitute and dependent upon the charity of her landlord,

George McGowan, Catherine Dennis filed for a mother's pension in the name of her deceased son. In arrears and without any means to support herself, Catherine was granted $8 a month from the United States Pension Office. William Dennis was only 22-years-old at the time of his death.

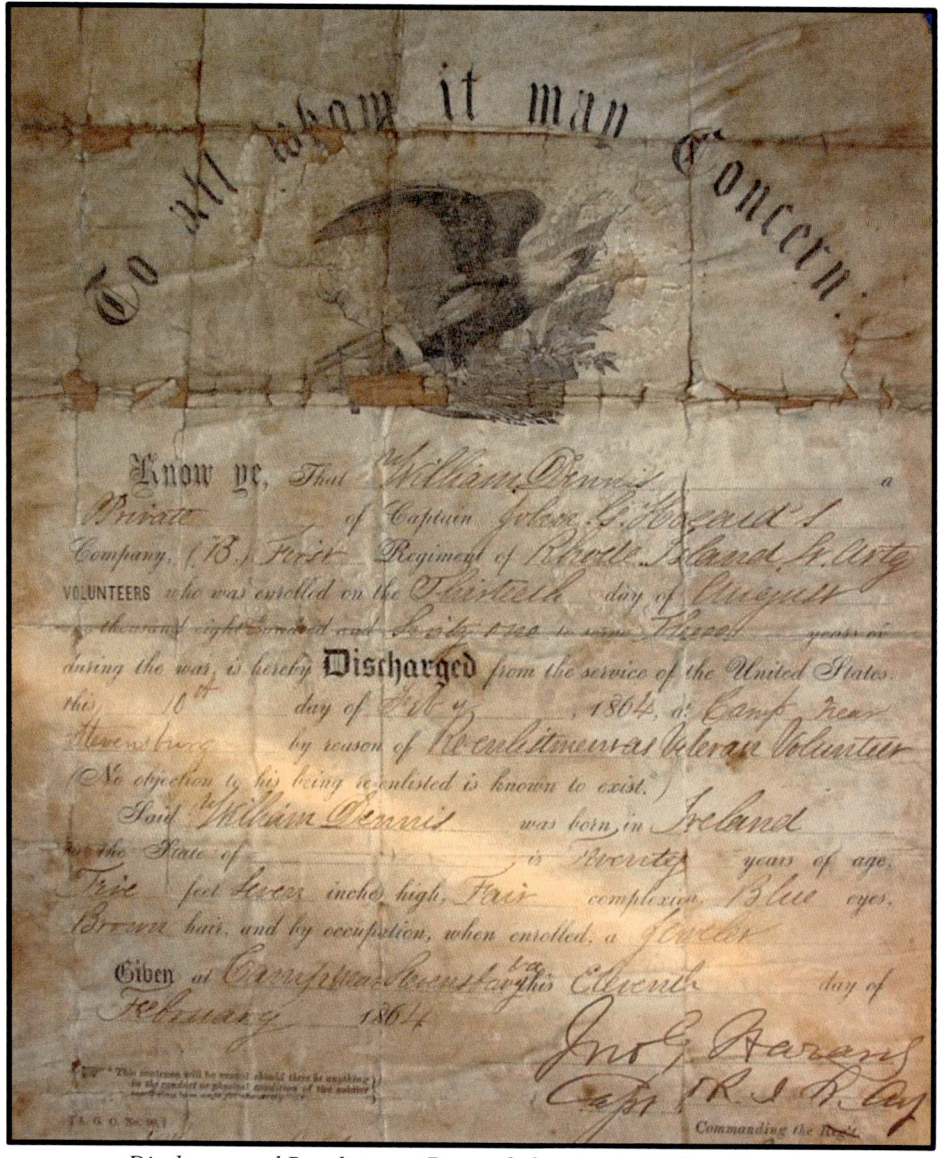

Discharge and Reenlistment Papers belonging to William Dennis

Notes:
1. John H. Rhodes, *The History of Battery B, First Regiment Rhode Island Light Artillery* (Providence: Snow and Farnum, Printers, 1894), 265, 278
2. Case Files of Approved Pension Applications of Widows and Other Veterans of the Army and Navy Who Served Mainly in the Civil War and the War with Spain, compiled 1861–1934, National Archives, Washington D. C. WC31814-DENNIS-William
3. Photo and Discharge Papers courtesy of the Battery B First Rhode Island Light Artillery Inc. Collection

ALBERT MORRIS

8

The Quarrel

Albert Morris was born in 1842 in Quebec, Canada. In September 1862, at the age of 20, he enlisted in the 12th Rhode Island Volunteers, Company C. Morris saw action at Fredericksburg, Virginia in December 1862, where the 12th Rhode Island Volunteers were exposed to heavy musket and artillery fire as they advanced toward the stone wall at Marye's Heights. By the day's end, they would suffer a significant number of killed and wounded soldiers. Morris fell ill in the winter of 1863 and was in the hospital from March to July 1863. He was mustered out of service on July 29, 1863. On February 15, 1865, Albert Morris and his brother, Charles Morris, re-enlisted with Battery B First Rhode Island Light Artillery and remained with the Battery until the close of the war.

Forty-four years later, 67-year-old Albert Morris was living as a resident in Pavilion D of the Bristol Soldiers Home in Rhode Island. Living in that same pavilion, was another civil war veteran, 75-year-old James McKenna, who served as a bugler with Battery E First Rhode Island Light Artillery. McKenna stood five foot five inches tall and was described as a quiet man with a full head of white hair and a smooth-shaven face. He was a fairly new resident who had arrived at the home in 1908. Despite their common experience in the war and having served in the same Rhode Island regiment, Morris and McKenna did not see eye to eye.

At five o'clock in the morning on Friday, May 7, 1909, Morris and McKenna were locked in a heated quarrel. Witnesses would later say that the argument had actually started the night before and spilled into the next morning. At one point during the argument, Morris said in a contemptuous way that at least he never served time in state prison. The argument escalated and turned into a physical tussle. Morris, the larger and more powerful of the two, tossed McKenna to the floor. As he hit the ground, McKenna's eyeglasses cracked and cut his face.

McKenna got up, dusted himself off and, went back to his room while Morris went to the lavatory. McKenna then returned a few minutes later and waited outside the lavatory door for Morris to exit. As Morris exited the bathroom, McKenna struck him over the head with a two-foot-long wooden stick. Morris sustained the blow and somehow did not lose consciousness. By 7:00 that morning, however, about an hour after being hit over the head, Morris passed out and started to have convulsions. Head nurse, William B. Parker, was called to his room. There, Parker found a pitiful sight. Morris was lying on his bed in obvious pain unable to get up.

As Parker took his vital signs, he noticed that Morris's pulse was weak, had a significant size lump on his head and, was suffering from paralysis on his right side.

The nurse applied cold packs to his head and gave him an injection of strychnine. Still, Morris writhed in pain and became more restless as the hours went on. At one point he was muttering in both English and French, *"My God, I am suffering."* By 10:00 that morning, seeing no improvement, Parker had Morris moved to the hospital. Dr. Merriman, the Bristol Home house physician, went to the hospital to attend to his patient. When he arrived, he observed that the situation was much graver than he had initially believed. At 1:00 in the afternoon, despite various treatments, Morris died. The autopsy would later reveal that he died as a result of a *"concussion of the brain, meningeal congestion and, cerebral hemorrhage."*

The police were called to the Bristol Soldiers Home to respond to the incident where witnesses gave a statement and the wooden stick was turned over to police as evidence. John McKenna, however, was nowhere to be found. He had quickly and quietly slipped out of the soldier's home in an attempt to evade the local authorities. Later that afternoon, however, under Police Chief John H. Morrisey, local police found McKenna hiding in the woods on the edge of the Bristol town line. By 6:00 that evening, he was apprehended, arrested and, arraigned before Justice of the Peace George Peck on a dangerous assault charge. Through his attorney, McKenna pled not guilty and was incarcerated pending his trial.

That same evening, Morris's son Alfred Morris, was called to the police station and was told the news of his father's death. The next morning, Alfred went to the morgue to identify the body. He told police that though he had not seen his father in more than six years, the body was positively that of Albert Morris. On the same day, police officially notified John McKenna that Morris had died. McKenna replied coolly, *"It's too bad, but it can't be helped."*

News traveled fast of Morris's passing. By the evening of Saturday, May 8, 1909, several Battery B veterans became aware of their comrade's sudden death. That night, Charles Tillinghast Straight, Secretary of the Battery B Veteran Association, wrote a heartfelt condolence letter to the veteran's son, Alfred Morris. Enclosed with the condolence letter was a silk American flag and streamer to be used during the funeral ceremony.

Flag given to Alfred Morris by Charles Tillinghast Straight for the funeral service of Albert Morris

Three days later on May 11, 1909, Reverend Thomas J. Gillan officiated Morris's funeral service which was held at Saint Mary's Church in Bristol, Rhode Island. John McKenna remained in jail until his trial took place in November 1909. Judge Lee, of the Providence Superior Court, heard the case. After hearing from three witnesses, the court found McKenna guilty of murder. McKenna's attorney pleaded for leniency on account of McKenna's old age, the provocation of the act, and his honorable time in service during the Civil War. Taking these considerations into account, Judge Lee sentenced McKenna to one year in state prison. Albert Morris is buried in Saint Mary's Cemetery in Bristol, Rhode Island.

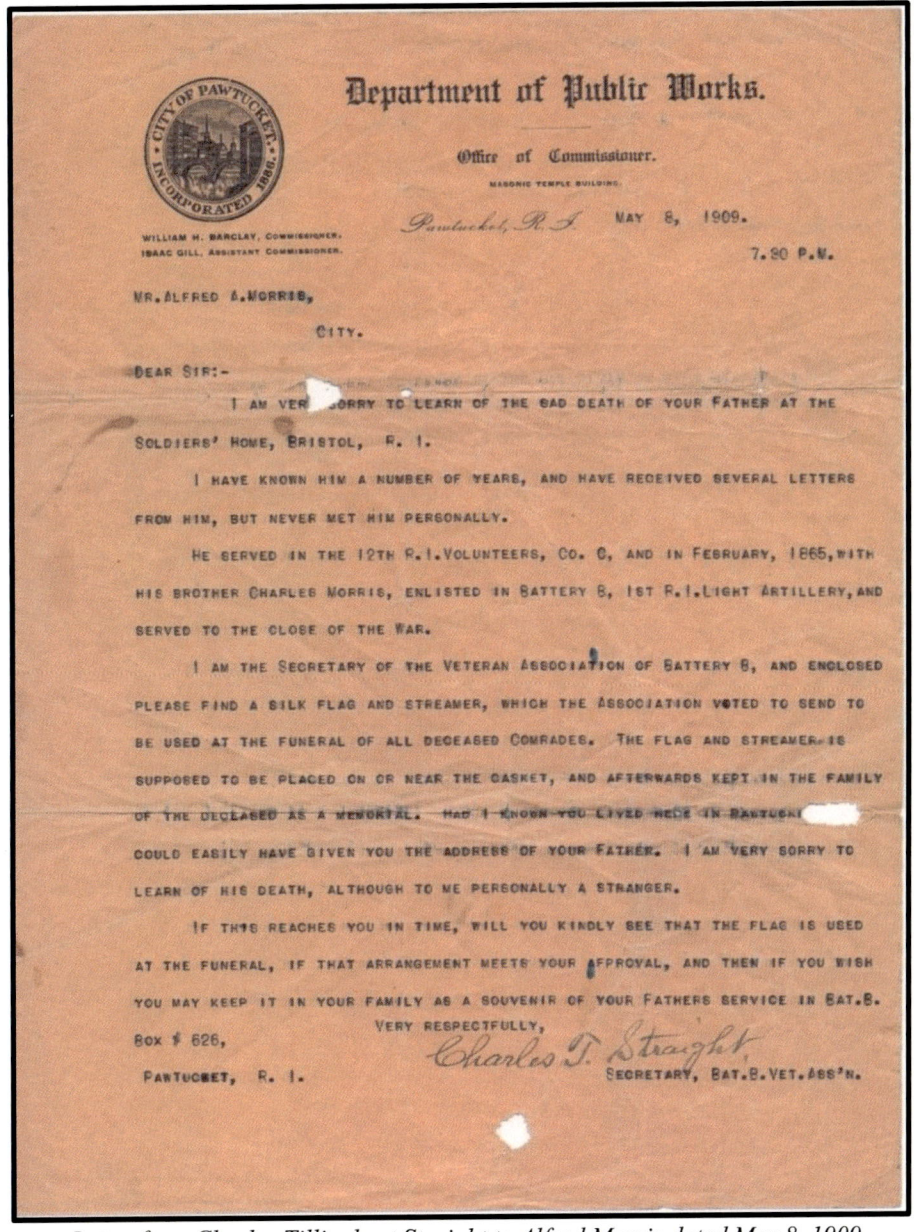

Department of Public Works.

Office of Commissioner.
MASONIC TEMPLE BUILDING.

Pawtucket, R.I. MAY 8, 1909.

7.30 P.M.

WILLIAM H. BARCLAY, COMMISSIONER.
ISAAC GILL, ASSISTANT COMMISSIONER.

MR. ALFRED A. MORRIS,
   CITY.

DEAR SIR:-

 I AM VERY SORRY TO LEARN OF THE SAD DEATH OF YOUR FATHER AT THE SOLDIERS' HOME, BRISTOL, R.I.

 I HAVE KNOWN HIM A NUMBER OF YEARS, AND HAVE RECEIVED SEVERAL LETTERS FROM HIM, BUT NEVER MET HIM PERSONALLY.

 HE SERVED IN THE 12TH R.I. VOLUNTEERS, CO. C, AND IN FEBRUARY, 1865, WITH HIS BROTHER CHARLES MORRIS, ENLISTED IN BATTERY B, 1ST R.I. LIGHT ARTILLERY, AND SERVED TO THE CLOSE OF THE WAR.

 I AM THE SECRETARY OF THE VETERAN ASSOCIATION OF BATTERY B, AND ENCLOSED PLEASE FIND A SILK FLAG AND STREAMER, WHICH THE ASSOCIATION VOTED TO SEND TO BE USED AT THE FUNERAL OF ALL DECEASED COMRADES. THE FLAG AND STREAMER IS SUPPOSED TO BE PLACED ON OR NEAR THE CASKET, AND AFTERWARDS KEPT IN THE FAMILY OF THE DECEASED AS A MEMORIAL. HAD I KNOWN YOU LIVED HERE IN PAWTUCKET COULD EASILY HAVE GIVEN YOU THE ADDRESS OF YOUR FATHER. I AM VERY SORRY TO LEARN OF HIS DEATH, ALTHOUGH TO ME PERSONALLY A STRANGER.

 IF THIS REACHES YOU IN TIME, WILL YOU KINDLY SEE THAT THE FLAG IS USED AT THE FUNERAL, IF THAT ARRANGEMENT MEETS YOUR APPROVAL, AND THEN IF YOU WISH YOU MAY KEEP IT IN YOUR FAMILY AS A SOUVENIR OF YOUR FATHERS SERVICE IN BAT. B.

       VERY RESPECTFULLY,

Box # 626,
PAWTUCKET, R.I.
       Charles T. Straight
       SECRETARY, BAT. B. VET. ASS'N.

Letter from Charles Tillinghast Straight to Alfred Morris dated May 8, 1909

Albert Morris grave, Saint Mary's Cemetery, Bristol, Rhode Island.

Notes:
1. John H. Rhodes, *The History of Battery B, First Regiment Rhode Island Light Artillery* (Providence: Snow and Farnum, Printers, 1894) 370
2. Oscar Lapham, *Soldiers and Sailors Historical Society of Rhode Island, Personal Narratives, Third Series, Nos. 11 to 20* (Providence Press Company, Printers, 1885) 36
3. The Bristol Phoenix, May 11, 1909 Page 1, Community History Archive, Bristol, Rhode Island, http://bristol.advantage-preservation.com/viewer/?k=james%20mckenna&i=f&by=1909&bdd=1900&d=0101190912311909&m=between&ord=k1&fn=bristol_phoenix_usa_rhode_island_bristol_19090511_english_1&df=1&dt=7
4. The Bristol Phoenix, May 21, 1909, Page 1, http://bristol.advantage-preservation.com/viewer/?k=james%20mckenna&i=f&by=1909&bdd=1900&d=0101190912311909&m=between&ord=k1&fn=bristol_phoenix_usa_rhode_island_bristol_19090521_english_1&df=1&dt=7
5. The Bristol Phoenix, May 25, 1909, Page 1, http://bristol.advantage-preservation.com/viewer/?k=albert%20morris&i=f&d=01011900-12311910&m=between&ord=k1&fn=bristol_phoenix_usa_rhode_island_bristol_19090525_english_1&df=1&dt=10
6. The Bristol Phoenix, November 9, 1909, Page 1, http://bristol.advantage-preservation.com/viewer/?k=albert%20morris&i=f&d=01011900-12311910&m=between&ord=k1&fn=bristol_phoenix_usa_rhode_island_bristol_19091109_english_1&df=21&dt=30
7. https://babel.hathitrust.org/cgi/pt?id=loc.ark:/13960/t6736wr9w&view=1up&seq=479&q1=Albert%20Morris
8. Photo of Albert Morris and Letter to Alfred Morris courtesy of the Battery B First Rhode Island Light Artillery Inc. Collection
9. *Find a Grave*, database and image (https://www.findagrave.com: accessed 11December 2020), memorial page for Albert Morris (unknown-7 May 1909), Find a Grave Memorial no. 206801976, citing Saint Mary's Cemetery, Bristol, Bristol County, Rhode Island, USA; Maintained by Elaine (contributor 47932173)

WILLIAM SMITH PERRIN

9

A Lonely Grave

Thirty-six hours had passed without food or water and his body was beginning to experience the effects of dehydration and exhaustion. But for the young lieutenant, that was the least of his worries. For the last day and a half, Lieutenant William Smith Perrin lay in the rain with a shattered leg below the knee.

Lying in the mud and unable to move, he could feel his broken shin bone and see the muscles and ligaments dangerously exposed. There was nowhere to go. Though it must have seemed like months enduring the agonizing pain, it was only the day before on August 25, 1864, that Perrin had been in command of his two-gun section at Ream's Station, Virginia. The fighting was horrendous, and Battery B suffered heavy casualties. During the battle, a hot shell fragment ripped into Perrin's leg carrying away part of his fibula. A nearby sergeant rushed to his side and carried him behind the Union lines where Perrin remained until Confederate forces overtook Battery B's position. When the battle was over, more than 48 men from the Battery were taken, prisoner. Perrin was one of them. In the rain, though feverish and weak, Perrin closed his eyes and waited. His thoughts drifted through the three years he had spent at war. For a young officer, Perrin had seen a lot.

The son of Dr. Nelson and Mary Jane Smith Perrin, William enlisted in the newly organized Battery C First Rhode Island Light Artillery as a corporal on August 25, 1861. He was quickly made a sergeant early in 1862 and performed bravely in battle at places like Mechanicsville, Malvern Hill, and Antietam. On November 11, 1862, he was made a second lieutenant with Battery B First Rhode Island Light Artillery and later promoted to first lieutenant on March 20, 1863. Through his service, Perrin was well respected and trusted by his superior officers and subordinates alike. His men described his demeanor as faithful, brave, loyal, and cool. Perrin had performed dozens of selfless acts to protect his men, whether on long marches or in the heat of battle, and they knew it. He was regarded as a true gentleman who always practiced modesty and compassion despite the tribulations he endured as a soldier.

Now languishing in the mud at Ream's Station, as the long hours passed in the torrential rain, Perrin endured the horrible tribulation and pain of splintered bones and blood loss but struggled nonetheless to hang onto consciousness. He was no stranger to the brutality of war. That brutality was omnipresent at Gettysburg. During the battle, Lieutenant Perrin had no sooner dismounted his horse in a storm of shells violently bursting around him, when a solid shot bounced off the ground and disemboweled the poor animal, leaving the horse's abdomen and stomach fatally exposed. As the animal took its last breath, Perrin surveyed his surroundings.

The air was thick with the smell of sulfur and smoke. Union artillerists were poised all along Cemetery Ridge, waiting to return a murderous fire as more than 100 Confederate cannons unleashed their fury on the Union lines. Despite the stress and anxiety of such a scene, Perrin was composed and calm. And he had to be. As its most senior officer, Perrin was now in command of Battery B's four guns on July 3, 1863 at the commencement of the Confederate's final artillery barrage that preceded Pickett's charge at Gettysburg. It was on July 2nd, 1863. Battery B's commanding officer, Fred Brown, had been shot in the neck and taken off the field. The intrepid twenty-four-year-old Lieutenant William Perrin, whose coolness and bravery no doubt, was observed by his men, did all he could to maximize the Battery's firepower aimed at Lee's Confederate lines. It would prove to be a grisly day. At just about 2:45 in the afternoon, after more than almost two long hours of continuous cannonading, Perrin was forced to relieve the Battery from the ridge. Out of ammunition and with men and horses scattered wounded and dead among the artillery pieces, Perrin was ordered to move the Battery to the protection of the Union rear.

William Smith Perrin on horseback

Fourteen days after the battle at Gettysburg, on July 17, 1864, Perrin penned a heartfelt correspondence from Battery B Headquarters in Sandy Hook, Maryland, to First Lieutenant Fred Brown who was recovering from his near-fatal wounds. In the letter, Perrin shares a first-hand account of the battle and relates the news of the severe losses suffered by the Battery. *"How any of us ever lived to get out of it alive seems a mystery"*, Perrin wrote, revealing his most intimate thoughts and feelings about the experience. Though exhausted and weary, Perrin took the time to inform Brown about the well-being of his beloved buckskin horse, who was also wounded when Brown was shot. The horse had been left behind at a nearby farm in Pennsylvania to recover. Perrin closed his letter with the following, *"Both men and horses are about used up."* Indeed, Battery B had been pounded at Gettysburg but mostly survived the ordeal, thanks to Perrin's strong situational leadership.

In late August 1863, despite the horrendous losses at Gettysburg, Perrin was ordered to march his men to the Union's Division Headquarters to witness the execution of three army deserters. Soldiers were often forced to witness such events to prevent them from deserting and re-enlisting under an assumed name for another monthly salary. The executions went horribly wrong and Perrin witnessed the mishandled killings of three young soldiers as the marksmen nervously aimed and missed hitting the necessary kill shots. Eventually, the deserters were put to death, but this event no doubt left an impression on the compassionate and kind officer.

Our Story

In October 1863, Perrin was slightly wounded in the foot at Bristoe Station but was largely unharmed. Despite the atrocities he witnessed and being wounded, he re-enlisted in the winter of 1864 for another three years. As an incentive, the Army of the Potomac granted Perrin a 35-day furlough to return home. On February 9, 1864, Perrin briefly went home to Rhode Island and then returned to the Battery on March 25, 1864 and spent the winter and spring with the Battery. On July 7, 1864, Perrin was transferred to Battery A First Rhode Island Light Artillery for about a month and a half and then returned to Battery B on August 18, 1864. Seven days later, Perrin would be desperately clinging to life in his blood-soaked uniform as the rains turned the ground around him to mud at Ream's Station.

Perrin was eventually taken prisoner by the Confederate forces and transferred to Libby Prison in Virginia. While imprisoned, doctors performed a hasty and bungled amputation on his shattered leg. The crude and ill-executed operation only exacerbated his pain, and Perrin would spend the next nineteen days lying on the crowded, flea-infested floors of Libby Prison before he was eventually paroled on September 12, 1864. Once released, Perrin was put in the care of Union doctors, who tried to treat his pain, but unfortunately, his leg would be an unending source of agony for the rest of his life.

A few weeks before Christmas in 1864, William Perrin was made a Brevet Captain of Battery B on account of his bravery and valor throughout his service. On February 4, 1865, Perrin was formally discharged from the Union Army on account of his disability. Despite his discharge, Perrin stayed in Virginia, likely still recuperating from his wounds. On the afternoon of May 19, 1865, he summoned the energy to visit his men in camp. When Perrin appeared, bereft of a leg, but not broken in spirit, the men wildly applauded the return of their beloved officer. They told him that just thirteen days earlier, Battery B stood before the now empty Libby Prison with its doors wide open. Former slaves greeted the Battery telling them that everyone was gone. There's no doubt, Perrin took some solace in knowing that the prison, where he endured such torture, was now a thing of the past. A little more than a month later, Battery B was mustered out of the federal service on June 13, 1865. For many, it would be the last time they would see Lieutenant Perrin alive.

Perrin returned home to Pawtucket, Rhode Island in June 1865. He took up residence on School Street in Providence where he rented a room in a boarding house owned by Mrs. Ester Gaylord. He eventually found work as a clerk at the Joseph Smith Company. In the early morning hours of August 13, 1876, (the 15th anniversary of the organization of Battery B), a young servant girl climbed the stairs of the boarding house and knocked on the door to Perrin's room. Like most mornings, she was about to inform him that breakfast was being served. After several attempts at knocking and receiving no response, the young girl opened the door to find Perrin still in his bed. When she tried to wake him, she noticed he was not breathing. Perrin was dead. Doctors determined he had died from a morphine overdose, which likely occurred as Perrin struggled to self-treat his gnawing pain. Unmarried and without any children, Perrin was buried in a small plot on the edge of a wooded area near Wilbur Road in Lincoln, Rhode Island. His headstone read-only, 'William Smith

Perrin'. Over many years, the small cemetery with a few scattered graves was swallowed by dense underbrush. Perrin, who had served his country and Battery B so honorably, was almost entirely erased from memory. More than three decades later in 1913, a veteran of Battery B First Rhode Island Light Artillery happened to stumble across the forgotten cemetery while out on an afternoon walk. Kneeling to see the broken headstones, he caught a glimpse of an old name that brought back an onslaught of memories; the name of William Smith Perrin. The old veteran related his discovery of the lonely and abandoned gravesite to the members of the Battery B Veteran Association. The Association's Secretary, Charles Tillinghast Straight, (son of Sergeant Albert Aaron Straight of Battery B), ventured out to the gravesite and, having found the stone amid the weeds, placed a small American flag in honor of the fallen soldier. Knowing that something more significant had to be done, Tillinghast wrote a letter to the Town Clerk of Lincoln, Rhode Island, requesting if William Perrin had any living relatives and recounted the deceased soldier's actions at Gettysburg. Upon receiving the short letter, the Town of Lincoln, R.I., eventually put Charles Tillinghast Straight in contact with Perrin's only surviving relative, his uncle, Mr. Seba Perrin.

Together, Perrin's uncle and Battery B veterans re-interred Perrin's body from his original burial site to a new gravesite at the Riverside Cemetery in Pawtucket, Rhode Island where Perrin lies today. It was a suitable, fitting, and proper conclusion for a fine soldier. In the end, it would take a little more than 36 years to re-discover William Smith Perrin, the young man who had suffered alone in the pouring rain for nearly 36 hours. He was 36 years old when he died.

Letter from Straight to the Town of Lincoln, Rhode Island

Grave of William Smith Perrin, Riverside Cemetery, Pawtucket, Rhode Island

Notes:
1. John H. Rhodes, *The History of Battery B, First Regiment Rhode Island Light Artillery* (Providence: Snow and Farnum, Printers, 1894) 214, 234, 265, 267, 307, 323, 347
2. Amos B. Carpenter, *A genealogical history of the Rehoboth Branch of the Carpenter family in America, brought down from their English ancestor, John Carpenter, 1303, with many biographical notes of descendants and allied families, Volume 1* (Amherst, MA: Carpenter and Morehouse, 1898), 267
3. http://ricemeteries.tripod.com/ln_ceme.HTM
4. Perrin, William Smith. Letter to Fred Brown. 17 July 1863. Courtesy of Mark McWorther Collection
5. Straight, Charles Tillinghast. Letter to the Town Clerk of Lincoln. 28 July 1913. First Rhode Island Battery B Light Artillery Inc. Collection
6. All photos courtesy of the First Rhode Island Battery B Light Artillery Inc. Collection

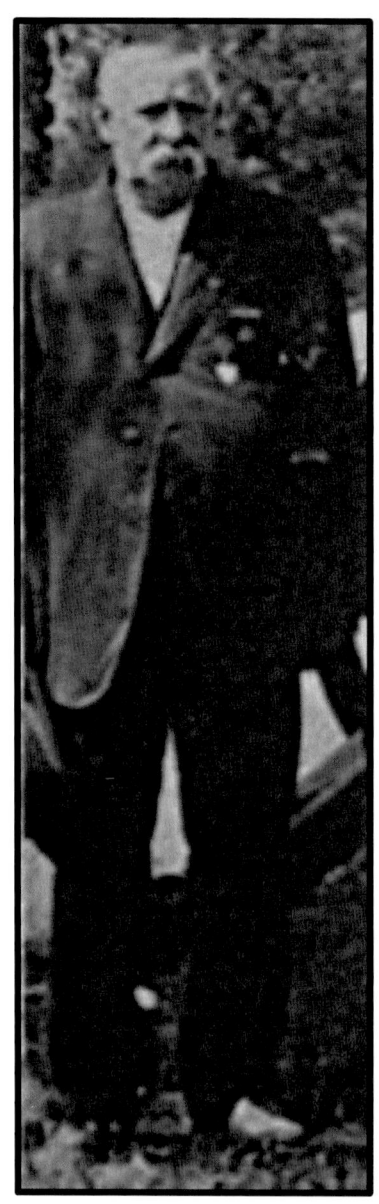

NAPOLEON BONAPARTE CLARKE

10

The Napoleon of Battery B

Napoleon Bonaparte Clarke was one of the original members of Battery B First Rhode Island Light Artillery enlisting as a corporal on August 13, 1861, at the age of 19. About a year later, Clarke was demoted to the rank of private for a "breach of discipline." Despite the demotion, Clarke served bravely in every battle and campaign at places like Antietam, Fredericksburg, Mine Run, and at Gettysburg, where the Battery suffered horrendous casualties on July 3, 1863. Amazingly, Clarke was not listed among Battery B records as having ever suffered from illness or injury during his roughly three years of service during the war. He was mustered out of the Battery on August 12, 1864, just a couple of weeks before Battery B would be nearly annihilated at Ream's Station, Virginia.

Getting back home to Rhode Island after his discharge, however, would not be easy for Clarke. On the day he was scheduled to return home, he almost missed the boat that would sail him back to Washington, DC on account of a technicality in his military paperwork. Eventually, the error was resolved and Clarke was able to reach Washington, DC, where he received his final soldier's pay. He then traveled home by train arriving at Exchange Place in Providence, Rhode Island.

Upon disembarking from the train, Clarke and his fellow comrades were met with a celebrating crowd of friends and family, who came to welcome them home. Clarke would later go on to marry Harriet Wood, and together they had four children. In 1913, Clarke traveled to Pennsylvania to attend the anniversary of the battle at Gettysburg along with his other comrades such as Gideon Spencer and George McGunnigle. Clarke would die one year later on November 17, 1914, at the age of 72. He is laid to rest at the North Burial Ground in Providence, Rhode Island.

Veterans of Battery B at the 50th Anniversary of the Battle of Gettysburg July 3, 1913

*Standing left to right: Napoleon B. Clarke, James H. Bowie, William T. Jordan, George McGunnigle, Joseph S. Nichols, Robert H. Cooper, George R. Matteson, Joseph S. Cassen
Sitting left to right: Charles H. Paine, John Mowry and Charles H. Bowden*

Discharge Papers belonging to Napoleon B. Clarke

Clarke grave at North Burial Ground, Providence, Rhode Island

Notes:
1. John H. Rhodes, *The History of Battery B, First Regiment Rhode Island Light Artillery* (Providence: Snow and Farnum, Printers, 1894) 362
2. http://www.ric.edu/northburialground/tours_civilwar-clarkenapoleon.html
3. *Find a Grave*, database and images, (https://www.findagrave.com: accessed 24 October 2020), memorial page for Napoleon B Clarke (1842 -1914), Find a Grave Memorial no. 11662791, citing North Burial Ground, Providence, Providence County, Rhode Island, USA; Maintained by Sons of the Union Veterans of the Civil War. Photo of grave by Jen Snoots.
4. Discharge Papers courtesy of the Clarke Family
5. Photos courtesy of the Battery B First Rhode Island Light Artillery Inc. Collection

JOHN TOWER BLAKE

11

"Old Geometry"

For a long while, he looked at his beautiful horses, all of them. He couldn't stand the thought of losing them, not one, not after how long he had bred them since he arrived in South Africa. The times were changing though and John Tower Blake knew it. He knew it when several English officers had approached his farm in Zeerust, South Africa, that hot afternoon. There was no denying the danger and the war that was erupting around his majestic ranch in the African countryside. The discovery of diamonds in the region ignited a war between the British Empire and the Boer States (the South African Republic and the Orange Free State). When the English officers finally knocked on the door, Blake politely let them in. Following her husband's lead, his wife Mariam proceeded to make some tea and invited the officers to sit down. There was no uncertainty about why they had come to visit Blake. They were there to enlist his help against the Boers, the farmers of German and Dutch descent, the early settlers of the area, who were now launching a type of guerrilla warfare against the English. As he sipped his tea and made small talk with the military envoys, Blake was silently thinking of what to do next. Through some twist of fate, Blake, who had fought and survived the bloody Civil War in America, had now found himself at war again.

John Tower Blake was born in Providence, Rhode Island on December 1, 1840. The son of George Emerson and Mary Johnson Blake, John attended public schools in Providence, Rhode Island, and later attended Brown University where he studied alongside classmate and friend, Thomas Fred Brown, who would later become Captain of Battery B First Rhode Island Light Artillery. A few months after the Civil War started, Blake left Brown University to enlist with the Union artillery. He was one of the 139 original members of Battery B First Rhode Island Light Artillery enlisting in Providence, Rhode Island on August 13, 1861. His enlistment began as sergeant and he was later made first sergeant on February 7, 1863. Blake was well liked amongst his fellow soldiers and earned the nickname "Old Geometry" because even in the heat of battle, Blake could figure out the trajectory of a shot or shell for a mile. In July 1863, Blake was badly wounded during the Battle of Gettysburg receiving a painful wound in the forearm. Amid the din of cannon fire and officers shouting orders, ambulance crews ushered Blake off the field to a nearby field hospital. After many months, Blake eventually recovered from his injuries and was promoted to Second Lieutenant of Battery A First Rhode Island Light Artillery four days after his 23rd birthday on December 5, 1863. He later received an honorable discharge on August 19, 1864, and went home to Rhode Island. Perhaps his time in the war and his many months in a Union hospital influenced Blake's decision when he returned to his residence in Providence. His experience as a soldier during the war would ultimately propel the young Blake to enroll at Boston's Harvard School of Medicine, where he ultimately earned his medical degree, almost three years later in 1867.

Upon his graduation, Blake practiced medicine in a small office close to his residence in Providence, Rhode Island. On July 4th, 1869, John traveled back to Gettysburg to visit an old friend, Sergeant Edwin A. Chase, who was the Assistant Engineer on the survey of the battlefield. Together, they rode on horseback over the entire battlefield, six miles long and almost five miles wide. They recalled all the vivid memories of the battle and those men he fought alongside in Battery B.

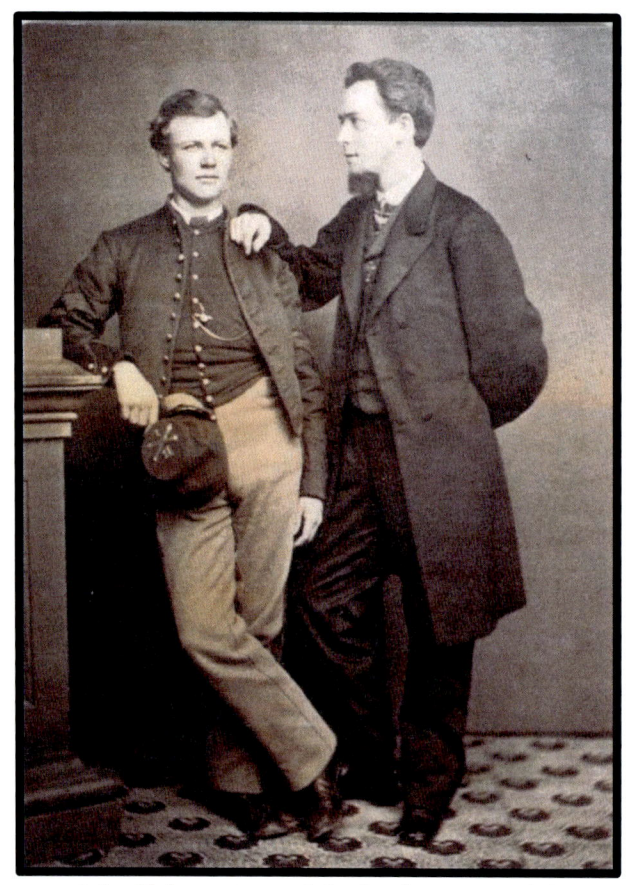

John Blake posing with his brother Lewis Blake

On December 14, 1870, 30-year-old John Blake married his first wife, 19-year-old Eleanor Curtis Aldrich in Providence, Rhode Island. Shortly after their marriage, the young couple set off in search of fortune in early 1871. The urge was irresistible. In 1867, diamonds had been discovered in South Africa and Blake was among the thousands of seekers who rushed to the continent in search of riches. John and Eleanor would have three children in South Africa, two daughters and one son. Blake's search for diamonds, however, did not pan out. After about a year of hunting and digging, Blake once again returned to his medical practice in South Africa this time, providing medical care to the Boers. After several years, John and Eleanor's marriage fell apart and the couple divorced. On May 23, 1882, John remarried his second wife, Mariam Blake Stroud, who was born and raised in Devonshire, England. Together they had one son, John Pitman Blake.

John and Mariam would lead a peaceful and serene life for many years on their ranch until 1899 when the Boer War broke out. Though he tried to avoid the conflict, Blake would inevitably be drawn into it and find himself face to face with English officers in his front parlor. The soldiers knew his wife, Mariam, was of

English descent and hoped they would be sympathetic to the English war effort in South Africa. As they gently put their teacups on the table and rose to their feet, they made their intentions known. They asked for all his horses and his entire supply of medicine.

He nodded politely and the English soldiers, assuming they had accomplished their objective, left his ranch. Blake glanced at his wife while his young son looked on from an adjacent room. He knew what he had to do. Blake waited several hours after the officers left and then walked out to his horse stables. There, the majestic animals ate from their troughs and neighed to each other in their stalls. Blake thought of the hundreds of draft horses he had tended to while in Battery B, their service in moving the caissons and guns, their bravery, and the suffering they endured in battle. He could not stand to think his horses would be forced to undergo such hardship under the English army. With a heavy heart and tears in his eyes, Blake shot each of his beloved horses one by one in the head. With each horse dead, he then blew up his entire medical dispensary sparing not one single bottle of medicine or treatment. With these heartbreaking actions behind him, he joined the Boer forces as a doctor and provided medical aid to the soldiers on the front. After the war, Blake would continue to practice medicine in Colesberg, Warrenton, and Transvaal, South Africa but he never forgot about his connection to Battery B.

On July 4, 1905, Blake penned a long letter to the Secretary of the Battery B Veteran Association, Charles Tillinghast Straight. In that letter, he asked Straight to relay a message to his old Battery comrades. John Blake tenderly wrote the following: *"And now of course, I will write something you can read to my old chums and comrades, dearer to me as the years roll on, and whom after many years of experience of life and men, I look back upon with ever increasing respect and esteem. Old comrades of Battery B, give me your hand, and if you were near enough, I would put my arm around your neck while we gossip of 'Auld Lang Syne' ye old fighting devils. If you had been with the Boers the English would have never got into this country. God Almighty has made some very good men, but he never made better soldiers than you, harmless, innocent looking old chaps. There is no egotism in feeling pride in our actions then, and thank God we have no cause to be ashamed of belonging to Battery B, ever after. Didn't we make ourselves known in both Armies? Wasn't we splendidly officered by such men as were complimented by both friends and foes? Didn't we always know we are going to do something worthwhile when 'stuttering Johnnie' or 'little Fred' took us into a fight? And what a set of trusty old war-dogs you became. All you required was to be put on the job-and then taken off when the time came...God bless each and every one of you and give you peace and contentment for the rest of the journey, and a smooth road to the end. Trusting that I shall meet you all on the road, I am with sincere regard and friendly greeting, Your old comrade, John T. Blake."*

In 1907, Blake's desire to see his old comrades came to fruition. Blake sailed 10,500 miles back to America to attend the Battery B Veteran Association's annual meeting at Boyden Heights in Rhode Island. It was the first time he had seen his old comrades in more than 30 years. That day, Blake shared in a warm reception and when it came time to elect a President of the Association at the close of the meeting, Blake was unanimously elected by a rousing vote.

Blake would return to South Africa and continue his medical practice until 1915. In early July of 1927, Blake fell ill and was hospitalized in Middelburg, South Africa. At 8:00 on the evening of July 22, 1927, Blake passed away from heart disease at the age of 86. He is buried in the European Cemetery, Middelburg, Transvaal, South Africa. His wife Mariam would live to age 90 and die on December 8, 1947.

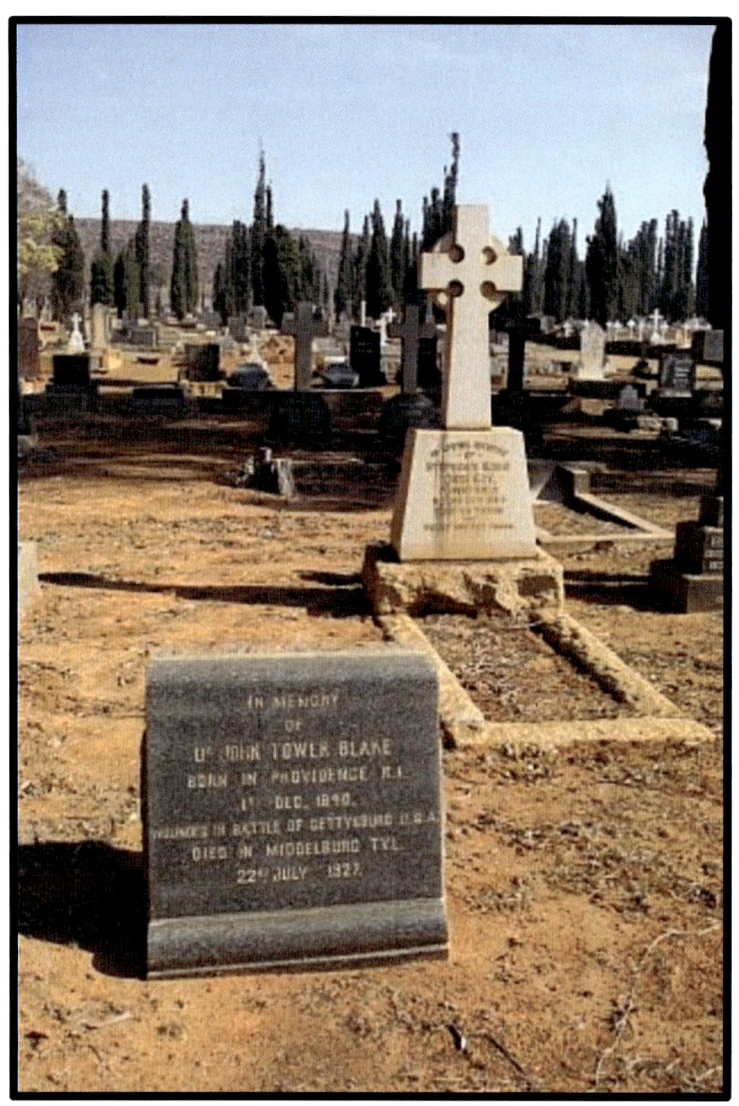

Grave of John Tower Blake, European Cemetery, Middelburg, Transvaal, South Africa

Notes:
1. "The Late Dr. John Tower Blake", Brown University Necrology, July 22, 1927
2. Straight, Charles Tillinghast. Letter to Fred Brown. 16 August 1905. Battery B First Rhode Island Light Artillery Inc. Collection
3. Chase, Edwin A. Letter to Charles Tillinghast Straight 6 January 1906. Battery B First Rhode Island Light Artillery Inc. Collection
4. John H. Rhodes, *The History of Battery B, First Regiment Rhode Island Light Artillery* (Providence: Snow and Farnum, Printers, 1894) 353
5. https://www.geni.com/people/John-Tower-Blake/6000000025125160872
6. Photo of John Tower Blake and his brother Lewis Blake, courtesy of the Mev Philips Collection
7. All other photos courtesy of the Battery B First Rhode Island Light Artillery Inc. Collection

EDWIN HOXSIE KNOWLES

12

"A Battery Cannot Live Out There"

At 3:45 on the afternoon of December 13, 1862, Edwin Hoxsie Knowles and his comrades were about to be sacrificed. Though they didn't know it at the time, Union commanders had decided that Battery B was worth slaughtering to remove the enemy's stubborn rifle pits from a sunken farm lane at the foot of Marye's Heights. During the murderous battle at Fredericksburg, where more than 12,000 Union soldiers were killed, Edwin and fifteen other young soldiers of Battery B would know exactly what that sacrifice meant.

Edwin grew up in a large family in Glocester, Rhode Island. He was born on February 18, 1842, the son of Dr. John and Catherine Knowles. At the age of 19, Knowles enlisted as a corporal in Battery B, as one of the original recruits on August 13, 1861. Though still a young man, Knowles had experienced the horrors of war up close. He was at the Battle of Ball's Bluff, fought through the Peninsula Campaign, and saw the destruction and death left behind at Antietam. The winter season of 1862 would bring more bloodshed for the brave soldier.

The morning of December 13th broke cold and ominous. Like many of his fellow artillerists, Edwin tried to hide the fire over which he made some coffee in an effort to avoid being shot. By mid-morning, Edwin was marching down Caroline Street amidst the rubble of shattered houses and buildings of Fredericksburg that had been shelled over the last several hours. Soon orders were shouted to mount the limber chests and march toward the front. Other batteries cheered Edwin and his comrades as they passed by, but they all knew they were heading directly into a hellish scene. By noon, the Battery had changed its position several times to avoid the deadly range of Confederate artillery raining down into the city.

Throughout the day, wave after wave of blue uniforms advanced over an open field only to be repulsed by merciless Confederate rifle and artillery fire. The stone wall, where several thick ranks of Confederates fired volley after volley, was nearly impenetrable. By 3:45 in the afternoon, thousands of young Union volunteers had been cut down and were scattered across the battlefield. It was determined at that point that additional artillery was needed to provide cover for another fresh division of infantry to take the stonewall. The decision was made to throw Battery B into the deadly chaos. The Federal commanding officers knew that this decision would have dreadful consequences. As the battle raged on, one of the captains shouted to General Couch, *"My God! General, you will lose your guns, a battery cannot live out there!" The General responded, "Then it can die there."* Within minutes, Edwin and the six-gun crews of Battery B moved into position within just 150 yards of the ferocious Confederate rifle pits. Over the next forty-five minutes, the Battery fought heroically though they suffered heavy casualties under horrific enemy fire. Artillery shells and shrapnel rained down on the young Union cannoneers. Several horses were hit and disemboweled. Still, the young men bravely stood their posts despite the withering fire. Within just a few minutes, three soldiers who took up the number one position at the muzzle of the gun had been mercilessly struck down. They continued to fire in quick succession, at one point, emptying all of their remaining ammunition chests. The drivers galloped back and forth to the caissons to resupply the Battery's dwindling ammunition.

Mini balls hissed and whizzed through the cold air hitting cannoneers in the hips, ankles, necks, wrists and groin. One of those balls would find its target, blowing a gaping hole into the left thigh of Edwin Knowles. Wounded but still alive, Knowles laid on the field until around 4:30 in the afternoon, when Battery B withdrew from the field as Union infantry tried again in vain to take the stone wall.

Edwin's fellow soldiers helped carry him and fifteen other wounded soldiers away from the front to an open lot on Caroline Street. From there, it's likely that Edwin endured the misery of an ambulance cart ride to one of the many
military field hospitals where he received initial treatment for his wounds. Within days, he would lay on a stretcher at one of Virginia's wharves to be transported 545 miles north via transport ship to Portsmouth Grove Hospital in Rhode Island. Edwin would spend the next couple of months recovering from his injuries. He would briefly return home to see his family before rejoining the Battery again. Edwin would never fully heal and was eventually mustered out of service on August 12, 1864. In the years after the war, Knowles would move to Westerly, Rhode Island where he would open his own drug store and then earn his doctorate degree in medicine. He married Mary Elizabeth Knowles (Champlin) and had one son. He would spend the rest of his life treating patients in North Stonington, Connecticut. Edwin Knowles died of kidney failure at his home on May 30, 1910. He was 68 years old. He is buried in River Bend Cemetery in Westerly, Rhode Island.

Edwin Knowles and family

Edwin Knowles is buried at River Bend Cemetery in Westerly, Rhode Island

Notes:
1. John H. Rhodes, *The History of Battery B, First Regiment Rhode Island Light Artillery (Providence: Snow and Farnum, Printers, 1894),* 137-145
2. Norwich Bulletin, May 31, 1910, Page 6, Image 6, Connecticut State Library, Harford, CT, *https://chroniclingamerica.loc.gov/lccn/sn82014086/1910-05-31/ed-1/seq6/#date1=1789&index=0&rows=20&words=Edwin+H+Knowles&searchType=basic&sequence=0&state=&date2=1963&proxtext=Edwin+H.+Knowles&y=15&x=13&dateFilterType=yearRange&page=1*
3. Damon, Laura, *Portsmouth hospital has surprising link to Civil War,* Updated January 10, 1019, *https://www.newportri.com/news/20190110/portsmouth-hospital-has-surprising-link-to-civil-war*
4. All photos courtesy of the North Stonington Historical Society Collection, Connecticut

JOHN F. LEACH

13

The Brave Musician

John F. Leach enlisted with the Second Rhode Island Volunteers as a musician at the age of 17 on June 5, 1861. Fifteen days later he was transferred to Battery A First Rhode Island Light Artillery. Though young with a boyish appearance, Leach went above and beyond his required duties as a bugler and distinguished himself as one of the bravest soldiers among the Rhode Island Batteries. For a little more than two months, John Leach was temporarily attached to Battery B First Rhode Island Light Artillery from September 10, 1863 to November 23, 1863. It was during that time that the Battery was engaged in a battle at Bristoe Station, Virginia on October 14, 1863. Leach was serving as Battery B's bugler and guidon bearer for First Lieutenant Thomas Fred Brown. During the battle, the men from Battery B found themselves separated from the support of the Union infantry and were left to face the onslaught of a Confederate ground assault. With little choice, the Battery opened fire on the enemy but, knew that it would just be a matter of time before Confederate soldiers would overrun their vulnerable position.

Seeing Battery B's dangerous predicament, John Leach mounted a Battery horse and rallied 13 stragglers (men from different Union divisions who were left on the field) pulling them all together into one cohesive unit. Brandishing his sword, he ordered the soldiers forward and assembled them into a makeshift skirmish line. His instinct and actions were perfectly timed. Just as the ragtag soldiers took their post by a nearby railroad, Confederate skirmishers began advancing, fire leaping from their muskets. Leach galloped up and down his line of men urging them on. The 13 men put up such a show of firepower that the Confederate soldiers were misled into thinking that there was a sufficient force of Union infantry behind Leach's small advance guard. Bullets hissed and whizzed by Leach as he shouted orders to his men. At one point, a bullet seemed to come out of the sky. It was at that moment that Leach turned to see a Confederate sharpshooter in a nearby tree. He ordered three of his men to take aim at the enemy sniper and take a shot. Within seconds, the Confederate sniper fell to the ground. For more than an hour, Leach kept his position and held on against advancing Confederate assaults until the Union infantry finally sent reinforcements to the field.

Leach remained on his horse throughout the rest of the battle until the poor animal was shot. As the horse went down, it landed on Leach nearly crushing him. Just as he was managing to break free from the injured horse, a shell fragment sliced into Leach's right leg. Still, he refused to leave the scene of the fight. He stayed until the battle was over and then had his wounds dressed by Sergeant Amos Onley of Battery A who sewed up the gash, preserving the young man's leg. Leach's horse was not so fortunate. The poor animal was so badly wounded that First Lieutenant Fred Brown ordered the horse shot and killed.

John F. Leach would go on to survive the battle at Bristoe Station and the war. He was mustered out of federal service on June 18, 1864. He lived until age 70 and died in 1914. He is buried in Saint Francis Cemetery, Pawtucket, Rhode Island.

Grave of John F. Leach, Saint Francis Cemetery, Pawtucket, Rhode Island

Notes:
1. John H. Rhodes, *The History of Battery B, First Regiment Rhode Island Light Artillery* (Providence: Snow and Farnum, Printers, 1894) 370
2. Thomas M. Aldridge, *The History of Battery A, First Regiment Rhode Island Light Artillery,* (Providence: Snow and Farnum, Printers, 1904) 254-256, 404
3. Augustus Woodbury, The Second Rhode Island Regiment, A Narrative of Military Operations, (Providence, Valpey, Angell and Company, 1875) 550
4. http://rigarcwmuseum.tripod.com/batteryahistorypage3.html
5. https://warfarehistorynetwork.com/2019/03/19/rebel-blunder-at-bristoe-station/
6. *Find a Grave,* database and images (https://www.findagrave.com: accessed 24 October 2020), memorial page for John F. Leach (1844–13 Mar 1914), Find a Grave Memorial no. 15581410, citing Saint Francis Cemetery, Pawtucket, Providence County, Rhode Island, USA; Maintained by Jen Snoots (contributor 4661415)
7. Photo of John Leach courtesy of Battery B First Rhode Island Light Artillery Inc. Collection

THOMAS FREDERICK BROWN

14

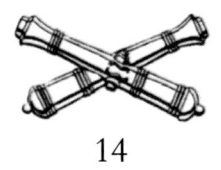

"I Am Indebted For My Life"

It was a surreal moment. At 3:00 in the afternoon of April 14, 1864, Sergeants Charles H. Adams and Charles A. Libbey asked First Lieutenant Thomas Fred Brown to come outside of his officer's quarters. When Brown emerged, he saw the men from Battery B assembled before him standing at attention in a perfectly straight line. As he glanced to his right, he observed the regimental band from the Fourth New York Heavy Artillery as they began playing a patriotic overture. A large number of officers from Battery B as well as Battery A stood at strict attention as the sun beat down on the assemblage. Brown looked out over the war-weary men of Battery B and could not help but think how he arrived at this moment.

Thomas Frederick Brown was born on October 26, 1842, in Providence, Rhode Island. He graduated high school and was in his third year at Brown University when the Civil War began in 1861. When Fred Brown initially enlisted in the First Rhode Island Regiment, he was rejected. The war recruiters told the young man that he was too short. Brown, however, would not be deterred and enlisted again as a corporal and was later made sergeant in Battery A on June 6, 1861. That fall, Brown fought at the First Battle of Bull Run and later that July at Malvern Hill when he had a sword shot out of his hand. On August 13, 1862, Brown was made Second Lieutenant in Battery C First Rhode Island Light Artillery and saw action at the Second Battle at Bull Run, Antietam and, Fredericksburg. He was promoted to First Lieutenant and reported for duty with Battery B in February 1863. At Gettysburg, on the afternoon of July 2, 1863, First Lieutenant Brown and his Battery were positioned at the very place where General Robert E. Lee launched a desperate attempt to break the Union lines on Cemetery Ridge.

The position of Battery B's cannons extended out further than any on the Union line, putting the Battery in a dangerous and exposed position. Under heavy fire and in danger of being captured, the 2nd Corps commanders ordered Brown to withdraw the Battery from the field. Brown, hearing the command, began the process of pulling his six guns back through a narrow gap in a nearby stone wall toward the protection of the Union lines.

Lieutenant Brown, wearing a white hat, and mounted on a wildly nervous buckskin or tan-colored horse, was galloping up and down the lines ordering his men. The sounds and chaos of the battle were overwhelming to the poor anxious horse, who had previously only served on an ambulance team. This was the horse's first time in battle. Sweating and covered in dust, the skittish horse almost looked roan or white in color. Sitting in the saddle of the dancing horse, Brown brandished his derringer pistol, shouting to his men to pull their cannons back behind the stone wall to prevent them from being captured. Bullets were flying everywhere as the Confederate infantry rapidly swept across the field. Brown had managed to get half of his Battery back behind the wall when Wright's Georgian Brigade suddenly appeared on top of the Battery's position.

Private David King and Lance Sergeant Henry Ballou were shot down as the Confederates advanced up the slope. As Brown was leaning forward on his horse and shouting to General Hazard of the 2nd Corps, one of the Confederate soldiers leveled his .58 caliber Enfield Rifle at near point-blank range and shot Brown in the neck. Brown lurched in the saddle, swayed and, then fell off his horse. In the confusion of the Battery's retreat, Brown was left for dead. As the daylight faded and the sounds of battle subsided, Brown, senseless and unconscious waited for the end to come. But the end did not come. After the battle, Brown was found and removed from the field. After being initially treated at a nearby field hospital, Brown was sent back to Rhode Island to recover from his wounds. The surgeons were able to save Brown's life by removing the bullet that had just missed his carotid artery. Four months later, Fred Brown was reunited with his beloved Battery. As a salute to their commanding officer, Brown fired the first round at Bristoe Station, Virginia on October 14, 1863. He would have command of Battery B once again during another tense battle at Mine Run in December 1863. Later in February 24, 1864, Brown left Battery B to become Adjutant of the First Rhode Island Regiment. Two months later on April 13, 1864, Brown would be brought back to Battery B and made Captain.

White hat worn by Brown on July 2, 1863 during the Battle of Gettysburg. A bullet cut away the small piece of the trim.

That next day on April 14, 1864, Brown would find himself standing before the entire Battery assembled in his honor. When the Fourth New York Heavy Artillery regimental band finished the last notes of its song, Battery B presented Captain Brown with a sword and belt. The sword's blade was adorned with emblematic designs and a metal sheath with an engraving of the Goddess of Liberty. The ivory handle was elegantly designed with an emblem of the cross cannons of the artillery and a gold eagle. Captain H.B. Goddard made the presentation and gave a short speech. He outlined Brown's honorable service, his numerous promotions, and his devotion to the Battery. At the end of his address, Goddard said, *"You return to us with the crowning wish of your and our hearts gratified, by your commission captain of your own best-loved battery, the non-commissioned officers and men of* its organization deem it a fitting opportunity to present a token of their esteem. In their behalf, I present you this sword and belt. Accept them, sir, as a fitting tribute from gallant men to a gallant officer."* With a sense of humility, grace and calm, Brown took the saber and belt in hand and addressed his men. *"My chief desire that I expressed to you two months ago on my departure has been granted, to be with you in the coming campaign. And my thanks shall be expressed in the making of every effort to prepare ourselves for the work before us and making then in the hope of drawing this saber in some crowning triumph - some second Gettysburg."* Three cheers rose from the ranks and the men celebrated with their newly minted Captain that afternoon. There would be no "second Gettysburg", but Brown would lead Battery B into crucial battles through the rest of the war at places like the Wilderness, Spotsylvania, Po River, North Anna, Cold Harbor and, Petersburg. In December 1864, Brown received another promotion, this time Brevet Major and later was made Brevet Lieutenant-Colonel on April 9, 1865. When Brown finally mustered out of federal service on June 12, 1865, he went home to Rhode Island as Lieutenant Colonel T. Fred Brown, First Rhode Island Light Artillery Battery B.

When the Civil War ended, Brown relocated to Cincinnati, Ohio and became a successful businessman. He married Alice Hill Brown and had two daughters. In 1896, thirty-one years after the war, Brown received a letter from the Providence Journal in Providence, Rhode Island. The letter was dated August 4, 1896, from a member of the 48th Georgia Regiment. Members of the 48th Georgia were documenting their role in the Battle of Gettysburg and one of them, Simeon Theus, wrote to the Providence Journal trying to ascertain if there were any living members of Battery B who could help them verify their position on the field in 1863. The Journal sent the letter to Captain Brown, who responded personally to Theus on September 8, 1896. In his letter, Brown recounted his role and that of Battery B at Gettysburg, stating that he was on a buckskin-colored horse, waving a pistol, trying to get his men off the field when he was shot in the neck. Two months later, on December 11, 1896, Simeon Theus wrote back to Brown. Theus wrote that Brown's letter was like the *"coming true of a dream."* Startled at what Brown's letter revealed, Theus asked Brown if he could recount in detail, the exact moments before he was wounded. In that same letter, Theus also described his experience at Gettysburg, telling Brown that he was part of the Georgian Brigade that advanced upon Cemetery Ridge on July 2, 1863. During the fight, Theus was hit in the groin and carried that metal shot in his body for 29 years before having it removed and made part of a watch chain he carried in his pocket as a reminder.

Brown wrote back to Theus a month later on January 20, 1897, providing additional details of his role in the battle including details of the moment he was shot. When Theus wrote back to Brown a couple of months later on March 23, 1897, he said that in the heat of the fight at Gettysburg, one of his comrades yelled out, *"Shoot that officer on the roan horse." Is it probable that you are the man?"*, Theus wrote.

Simeon Theus went on to confess, *"Now my dear friend, after telling this story for 30 years, you can imagine the dumbfounded credulity your first letter found me - twas like one from the dead. I know I fired upon an officer under those conditions, and at such close range I could not miss him. He fell from his horse; he was mounted on, as my friend cried out, a roan horse…Now you see, instead of you being the aggressor, I'm the man."*

Brown read Theus's letter several times with disbelief. After 31 years, he was now communicating with the man that had shot and nearly killed him. On June 18, 1897, Brown responded to Simeon Theus.

In his letter, Brown kindly wrote, *"It looks very much as though you are the man to who I am indebted for my life. By wounding me, severely on the late afternoon of the second no doubt kept me from being killed in General Pickett's charge on the third. For three Battery commanders were killed on the third…All the incidents you describe, fit perfectly. My battery was put out in front of the line. Expecting to be sent down to help Sickles line. The orders never came but you did. I had on a white hat…I trust we may be spared a few years more. When we shall surely meet."*

Brown and Theus, once enemies would become close, lifelong friends. They would go on to exchange numerous letters throughout the rest of their lives and attempted several times to meet in New England and Georgia. The timing and the conditions however never seemed to work out. They continued to communicate as late as 1909. In 1912, Simeon Theus passed away, ending the camaraderie that existed between the two soldiers who were once mortal enemies.

Fred Brown remained active in the Battery B Veteran Association and attended one of their reunions in 1916. Captain Thomas Frederick Brown died on November 27, 1928, in Daytona Beach, Florida. His wife Alice died on March 25, 1930. They are both buried at Swan Point Cemetery in Providence, Rhode Island.

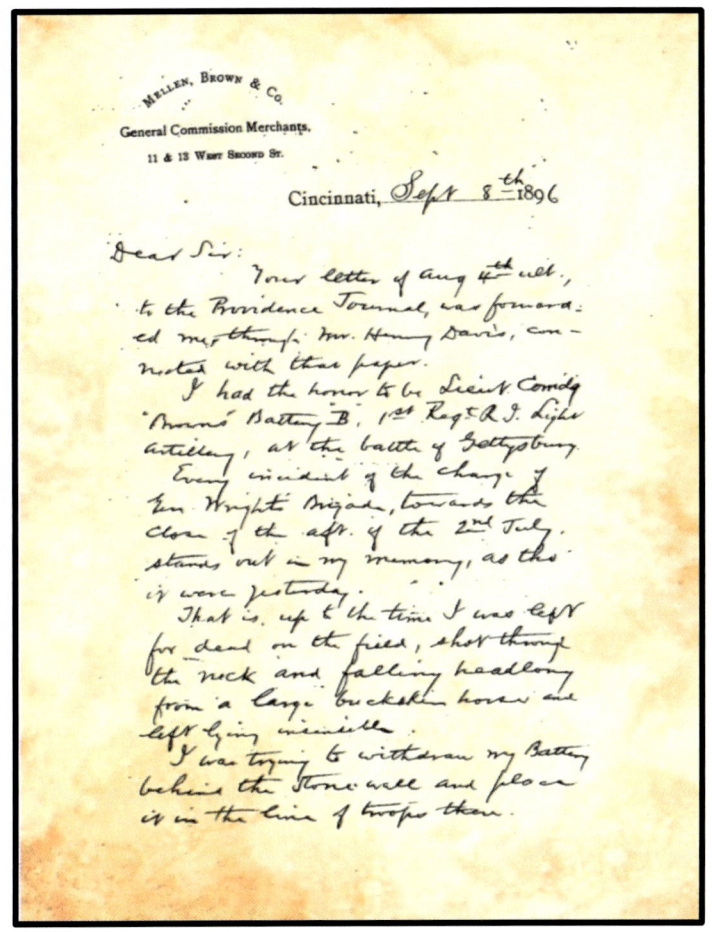

Letter from Fred Brown to Simeon Theus dated September 8, 1896

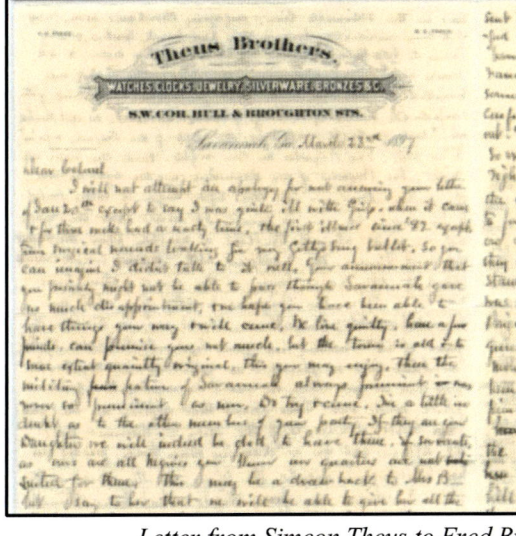

Letter from Simeon Theus to Fred Brown dated March 23, 1897

Fred Brown seated in the center row, fourth from the left at Battery B Reunion, June 18, 1916.

Colonel Fred Brown gravesite at Swan Point Cemetery, Providence, Rhode Island.

Notes:
1. John H. Rhodes, *The History of Battery B, First Regiment Rhode Island Light Artillery* (Providence: Snow and Farnum, Printers, 1894) 268-270
2. Theus, Simeon. Letter to Fred Brown. 4 August 1896. Courtesy of Mark McWorther Collection
3. Brown, Thomas Fred. Letter to Simeon Theus. 20 January 1897. Courtesy of Mark McWorther Collection
4. Brown, Thomas Fred. Letter to Simeon Theus. 18 June 1897. Courtesy of Mark McWorther Collection
5. Photos of Simeon and Brown letters courtesy of Mark McWorther Collection
6. Photo of Thomas Fred Brown, Brown Gravesite and Battery Reunion courtesy of Battery B First Rhode Island Light Artillery Inc. Collection

EBEN S. CROWNINGSHIELD

15

The Bugler

Eben S. Crowingshield was born in Hinsdale, New Hampshire on October 12, 1839. One of seven children, Crowningshield enlisted as one of the original members of Battery B on August 13, 1861, at the age of 22. He had the distinct honor of serving as Battery B's first bugler. While in camp, chief among his duties were to sound the calls for rolls, drills, camp inspections, and guard duty. While on long marches and in battle, Crowningshield would have been responsible for attending to the commanding officer, sounding the calls to march, to halt, to rest, strike the tents, and form up in battle. Bugle calls were critical during the war, as they could often be heard much better than the beating of drums over the thundering of artillery and musket fire. Crowingshield likely also served at times as a messenger, surgical assistant, and, on ambulance crews removing the wounded from the field of battle.

At Gettysburg on July 2, 1863, it would be Crowningshield who himself, would need the assistance of an ambulance crew. During the vortex of the battle, while sounding the critical bugle calls for First Lieutenant Fred Brown, Confederate infantry swarmed Battery B's position on Cemetery Ridge. Crowingshield was shot in the lung and fell wounded in the tall grass. Struggling to take a full breath, he was hastily removed from the field and brought to the rear, where surgeons believed his wound was mortal. Somehow, after several months, he survived and was eventually discharged from Battery B about a year later on August 12, 1864. Upon his discharge, he returned home to his native New Hampshire and in 1868 married Elizabeth S. Leach of Putnam, Connecticut. Together they would have five children. In 1878, the family relocated to Providence, Rhode Island and, moved into a small home on 8 West Clifford Street. Crowningshield would work as a foreman for the Household Furniture Company in Providence up until two years before his death. For the rest of this life, he was also an active member of the Battery B Veteran Association.

On Thursday, November 1, 1906, at the age of 67, Crowningshield passed away at his home from complications of the wound he received at Gettysburg. His funeral took place at his residence where Reverend Burgess, the pastor of South Baptist Church, conducted his memorial service. At the time of his death, he left behind his wife, Elizabeth, four boys and, one girl. He is buried at Walnut Cemetery in Pawtucket, Rhode Island.

Grave of Eben S. Crowningshield, Walnut Cemetery, Pawtucket, Rhode Island

Notes:
1. John H. Rhodes, *The History of Battery B, First Regiment Rhode Island Light Artillery* (Providence: Snow and Farnum, Printers, 1894) 358
2. Newspaper article (source unknown) dated November 6, 1906, courtesy of Battery B collection (Battery B Veteran Association)
3. *Find a Grave,* database and images (https://www.findagrave.com: accessed 24 October 2020), memorial page for Eben S. Crowningshield (unknown -1 Nov 1906), Find a Grave Memorial no.16481737, citing Walnut Hill Cemetery, Pawtucket, Providence County, Rhode Island, USA; Photo provided by Jen Snoots (contributor 4661415)
4. Photo of Eben Crowningshield courtesy of Battery B First Rhode Island Light Artillery Inc. Collection

JOSEPH STUART MILNE

16

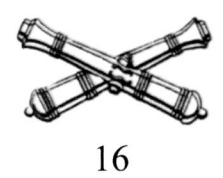

"Comfort My Mother When She Comes"

As the gray wave of thousands of Confederates rippled across the Emmitsburg Road on July 3, 1863, Lieutenant Joseph Stuart Milne, took a deep breath. Milne was no stranger to battle. At Fredericksburg in 1862, his horse was shot out from underneath him. Milne was young but resilient. Just days before the Gettysburg Campaign, Milne was detached to serve in Battery A, Fourth United States Artillery, better known as "Cushing's Battery". Milne, a highly respected and skilled officer from Battery B First Rhode Island Light Artillery, had been sent to assist Alonzo Cushing, whose Battery was in need of officers. Though he didn't know it at the time, as the Virginia brigades rapidly approached Battery A's position on Cemetery Ridge, Joseph Milne's short life was coming to an end.

Joseph Stuart Milne was born in Bolton, New York on April 27, 1842. He was the son of the Reverend Andrew Milne and Anna Tennant Milne. As a young man, Milne worked as a printer for one of his father's publications, the *Glen Falls Messenger*, which was a religious paper that was circulated in New York. When the Milne family moved to Fall River, Massachusetts, Milne worked for two years as a print setter at the *Daily News Office*. Milne later worked at the Providence *Daily Post* until the outbreak of the Civil War. When President Lincoln put out a call for volunteers, Milne enlisted in Battery E First Rhode Island Light Artillery as one of the Battery's first sergeants on September 30, 1861. A little more than a year later, he would be made 2nd Lieutenant in Battery B First Rhode Island Light Artillery.

From his position in Battery A at Gettysburg, Milne would have been able to see his Battery B comrades, perhaps fifty yards to his left, as the Battery worked its four serviceable guns. Milne, too, was working his two-gun section when a shell violently exploded and sent shell fragments into the shoulder and groin of Lieutenant Alonzo Cushing. Despite the gruesome wounds, Cushing stubbornly refused to leave his post. Cushing would eventually be killed when a bullet entered his head during the grueling ordeal moments later. Milne however, kept on his feet as the Confederates cascaded over the stone wall at the zenith of Pickett's Charge. The soldiers of Battery A fired their last rounds of canister and then used anything they could find as a weapon to defend themselves in hand-to-hand combat. Milne used his officer's sword while the other cannoneers used handspikes and rammers to defend the Battery's position and remaining guns. Milne fought bravely in the struggle until he felt a searing pain electrify his body. When he looked down, he noticed that he had been shot in the chest, the bullet piercing his left lung. Bleeding out, Milne was taken off the battlefield and moved to a field hospital behind the Union lines. The surgeons tended to the gaping hole in his chest. For several days, the twenty-year-old officer coughed up blood and struggled to take a full breath. By Wednesday, July 8, 1863, Milne's shattered lung and weakened body began to shut down. By that time, news of Milne's mortal wounds reached his horrified parents in Fall River, Massachusetts. His mother, Anna, had immediately set off on the 400-mile journey to Gettysburg to be with her dying son. Milne however, would not live long enough to see his mother arrive at his bedside.

The attending nurse told Milne that he likely only had a few hours to live. With eyes closed, Milne whispered to the nurse, *"Comfort my mother when she comes and tell her I died doing my duty."* Far from home, in the sweltering heat of the Pennsylvania countryside, Milne died a few hours before his mother arrived.

Under the attentive charge of Battery A's Lieutenant Lamb, Milne's body was brought home to Fall River, Massachusetts. Nine days after his death, on July 17th, Milne's casket was laid before the decorated altar of the Fall River Baptist Temple. The *Fall River News* evening edition wrote the following, *"The funeral services over the remains of this gallant young officer took place this afternoon at the Baptist Temple. A large congregation assembled, and the exercises, conducted by Rev. Charles A. Snow, pastor of the church, were very impressive."* The young man's body was dressed in his Union officer's blue uniform bearing the honored insignia of the First Rhode Island Light Artillery. Upon his casket lay his sword and an American flag draped with multi-colored flowers. The choir harmonized as they sang the sad words to the song, *"Put Me Down Gently, Boys."*

The papers in Rhode Island covered Milne's death with lengthy obituaries referring to Milne with great admiration, respect and praise for his service. Perhaps the highest praise however, came from General John Gardner Hazard who was the Captain of Milne's Battery and Chief of the Artillery in the 2nd Corps. In his report, Hazard wrote these words, *"Lieutenant Joseph S. Milne First Rhode Island Light Artillery, was mortally wounded on the afternoon of July 3rd, by a musket ball shot through the lungs. He survived his wound one week and breathed his last at Gettysburg...In his regiment he was known for his bravery and willingness to encounter death in any guise, while his modesty and manliness gained for him the ready esteem of his many comrades. His death is a loss to all, and we cannot but mourn that so bright a life should thus suddenly be veiled in death."*

The lives of the Milne family were shattered by the death of their son. Three years later in 1866, the Reverend Andrew Milne would die from a high fever leaving Anna Milne nearly destitute. She would go on to file a mother's pension in the name of her deceased son and receive a small monthly benefit. She would later die in 1895 at the age of 77, outliving her son by 32 years.

Lieutenant Joseph Stuart Milne is buried in Oak Grove Cemetery in Fall River, Massachusetts. He was the only Rhode Island officer killed during the battle at Gettysburg.

Headstone of Joseph S. Milne, Oak Grove Cemetery, Fall River, Massachusetts

Notes:
1. George Lewis, *The History of Battery E, First Rhode Island Light Artillery* (Providence: Snow and Farnum Printers, 1892) 120-121, 224-225, 490
2. https://armyhistory.org/i-will-give-them-one-more-shot-battery-a-4th-u-s-artillery-at-the-battle-of-gettysburg-2-3-july-1863/
3. John H. Rhodes, T*he History of Battery B, First Regiment Rhode Island Light Artillery* (Providence: Snow and Farnum, Printers, 1894) 214, 353
4. *Find a Grave*, database and images (*https://www.findagrave.com: accessed 24 October 2020*), memorial page for Lieut Joseph Stuart Milne (27 Apr 1843–7 Jul 1863), Find a Grave Memorial no. 68616628, citing Oak Grove Cemetery, Fall River, Bristol County, Massachusetts, USA; Maintained by GPoppa (contributor 46925364)
5. Photo of Milne courtesy of Battery B First Rhode Island Light Artillery Inc. Collection

JOHN EDWIN WARDLOW

17

Supporting the Union Cause

John Edwin Wardlow was born on Friday, October 16, 1840, in Pawtucket, Massachusetts (which is now a part of Rhode Island). His parents, James and Eliza (Cooke) Wardlow, had John educated in the Rhode Island public schools until 1861 when the Civil War erupted. John was adamant about supporting the Union cause and enlisted as a private with Battery B First Rhode Island Artillery on August 13, 1861.

Wardlow was disciplined, smart, and, performed excellent service as a soldier. He was promoted to sergeant in less than a year on December 15, 1861. Wardlow was present in all the major engagements where Battery B went into action between 1861-1863 including Gettysburg, where he served as Sergeant of the first piece under the command of Lieutenant William Smith Perrin. In October 1863, Wardlow became Second Lieutenant in the Rhode Island Volunteers, and later, First Lieutenant in December 1863. He also served as Quartermaster and Commissary from 1864-1865. In August 1865, Wardlow was discharged from service due to sickness. After returning home, he spent time in a New York hospital and later returned to Rhode Island to seek additional treatments for his health.

On March 10, 1867, while visiting family in New York City, John Wardlow died as a result of a sudden heart attack. He and his wife Eliza, are laid to rest at Oak Grove Cemetery, Pawtucket, Rhode Island. John was 27 years old at the time of his death.

John and Eliza Wardlow's grave at Oak Grove Cemetery, Pawtucket, Rhode Island

Notes:
1. John H. Rhodes, *The History of Battery B, First Regiment Rhode Island Light Artillery* (Providence: Snow and Farnum, Printers, 1894) 355
2. William H. Chenery, *The Fourteen Regiment Rhode Island Heavy Artillery Colored* (Providence, Snow and Farnum, Printers, 1898), 337
3. *http://civilwarthosesurnames.blogspot.com/2012/02/john-e-wardlow.html*
4. Photo of John Wardlow courtesy of Battery B First Rhode Island Light Artillery Inc. Collection

CHARLES AUSTIN BROWN

18

The Escape

As he languished in the dungeon prison for six weeks, Brown couldn't help but think, how history had a strange way of repeating itself. His grandfather, John W. Brown, a British soldier in the Revolutionary War, was also confined as a prisoner. After taking an oath of allegiance to the United States, the British Regular signed on to serve as a clerk to General George Washington. Charles Brown though had no intention of serving under General Robert E. Lee. Brown was in the fight of his life and he was determined to get out alive and rejoin the Union Army.

Charles Austin Brown was born on August 10, 1837, in Ironston, Massachusetts to parents Elisha and Pelthira (Hall) Brown. His family moved to Rhode Island when Charles was still a child and at age seven, he went to work in one of Rhode Island's many cotton mills. While working, Charles also attended schools in Providence and Burrillville and eventually graduated from Schofield's Commercial College. After graduation, Brown found employment painting houses and carriages and served as a member of Providence's City Horse Guard. Being tuned into the city's defense at the outbreak of the Civil War, Brown was especially keen on President Lincoln's call for volunteers and enlisted as a corporal with Battery E First Rhode Island Light Artillery, just seven days after the unit was organized on September 23, 1861. The young man was eventually promoted to quartermaster sergeant in March 1862 and then mustered as a second lieutenant a year later with Battery B First Rhode Island Light Artillery in March 1863. Four months later, Second Lieutenant Brown would find himself in command of Battery B's third and fourth guns at the Battle of Gettysburg on July 3, 1863. That afternoon, the muzzle of Brown's fourth 12-pound Napoleon gun was struck by a Confederate shell killing two of his artillerists. Sergeant Albert Straight rushed to load a solid shot into the dented cannon muzzle. As Straight struggled to ram the solid shot down the barrel with the rammer, Brown ordered one of the cannoneers to grab an axe from the caisson and give it to Straight to drive the shot down the tube. Even with an axe, the solid ball would not budge. Straight reported the piece disabled and the remaining Battery B cannoneers along with Lieutenants Brown and Perrin were retired from the field.

In May 1864, shortly after the Battle of Spotsylvania, Brown was responsible for transporting the captured Confederate cannons to the Union ordinance department depot in Belle Plain, Virginia. While making his way back to Battery B's encampment, Brown and several others were captured by Confederate John Singleton Mosby's cavalrymen known as 'Mosby's Guerrillas'. Confederate captors forced Brown to remove his uniform and transported him several times before finally confining him

Headstone of Charles Brown and his family, North Burial Ground, Providence, Rhode Island

Notes:
1. John H. Rhodes, *The History of Battery B, First Regiment Rhode Island Light Artillery* (Providence: Snow and Farnum, Printers, 1894) 210, 353
2. George Lewis, *The History of Battery E, First Regiment Rhode Island Light Artillery* (Providence: Snow and Farnum, Printers, 1892) 375
3. https://www.historynet.com/immortal-600-prisoners-under-fire-at-charleston-harbor-during-the-american-civil-war.htm
4. *Find a Grave,* database and images (https://www.findagrave.com: accessed 25 October 2020), memorial page for Charles Austin Brown (24 Jul 1837–5 Mar 1923), Find a Grave Memorial no. 30045773, citing North Burial Ground, Providence, Providence County, Rhode Island, USA; Maintained by Scout (contributor 47319613)
5. All photos courtesy of Battery B First Rhode Island Light Artillery Inc. Collection

GEORGE MCGUNIGLE

19

The Young Recruit

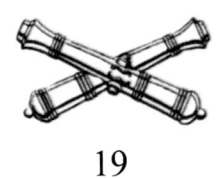

George Irving McGunigle was born on August 26, 1845, in Nova Scotia, Canada. The son of John and Mary Entwistle McGunnigle, he was the youngest of five children. When George was seven years old, his father, who worked as an innkeeper, suddenly died. Mary McGunnigle, with no means of monetary support, moved her young family to Providence, Rhode Island where she found work as a seamstress. At a young age, George worked as a spinner in the factories of Providence. At the age of 15 years old, the 5'7" tall teenager with hazel eyes and brown hair enlisted in Company G of the Rhode Island Detached Militia. Together with his brother, James, they both served in the chaotic Battle of First Bull Run.

When his initial three-month enlistment was over on August 2, 1861, George enlisted as an original member of Battery B First Rhode Island Light Artillery on August 13, 1861. At the time of his second enlistment, he was still almost a month shy of his sixteenth birthday. The young recruit would see harsh fighting in some of the largest engagements of the war, including Ball's Bluff, Yorktown, Fair Oaks, Malvern Hill, Antietam, Fredericksburg, Chancellorsville, and Gettysburg.

On the afternoon of July 2, 1863, McGunigle was serving as the Number 5 man on Battery B's third gun under the command of Sergeant Anthony Horton and Gunner Samuel Goldsmith during the battle at Gettysburg. With battle flags blowing in the breeze and artillery shells bursting, McGunigle was in the process of running ammunition from the limber chest to the cannon when he was wounded by flying shrapnel. His brother James, serving on the same gun, likely witnessed the injury and ushered his younger brother to safety behind Union lines. George McGunigle spent a full year recovering from his injuries. On June 17, 1864, he was transferred to the Veteran Reserve Corps, Company I. He would finally be mustered out of federal service on July 14, 1865. McGunigle would return home to Rhode Island after the war and marry Elizabeth Sparrow McGunigle in 1869. Together they had two sons, William Robert McGunigle in 1871 and Charles Foster

George McGunigle

McGunigle in 1878. McGunigle would find employment at the R. Bliss Manufacturing Company and work there for almost 45 years as a wood turner. On July 15, 1887, almost twenty years after being mustered out of federal service with the Battery, McGunigle became a naturalized citizen of the United States (note he spelled his last name with one "n").

He was also very active in Battery B's Veteran Association where he served as the President. In 1913, McGunigle traveled to Pennsylvania and was present at the 50th Anniversary of the Battle of Gettysburg. Three years later, at the age of 71, George McGunigle died at his home on 140 Garden Street in Pawtucket, Rhode Island. At the time of his death, he left behind his wife to whom he had been married for 47 years. The funeral service was held at his residence where Reverend George J. Bloomfield conducted the ceremony. In attendance were several members and associate members of Battery B. One such member, Bugler John Hickey, sounded "Taps" as McGunigle was gently lowered into his grave. Today both George and Elizabeth are buried at Oak Grove Cemetery in Pawtucket, Rhode Island.

Bugler John Hickey played at the funeral service for George McGunigle

United States of America

DISTRICT OF RHODE ISLAND

GREETING.

Be it Remembered, that at a ~~District~~ *Circuit* Court of the United States holden at Providence, within and for the District of Rhode Island, on the *15th* day of ~~December~~ *July*, in the year of our Lord ~~one thousand eight hundred and ninety-nine~~ *1887* *George McGunigle* of *Pawtucket* in said District, having produced the evidence, and taken and subscribed the oath required by law, was admitted to become a citizen of the United States, according to the Act of Congress in such case made and provided.

In Testimony Whereof, I have hereunto set my hand, and affixed the seal of said Court, at Providence aforesaid, this *22D* day of ~~December~~ *April*, A. D. ~~1899~~ *1905*, and in the one hundred and twenty-fourth year of Independence of the United States of America.

William P. Cross,
CLERK

By *Thomas Hope* Clerk.
DEPUTY CLERK.

Naturalization Certificate belonging to George McGunigle

Burial site of George McGunigle, Oak Grove Cemetery, Pawtucket, Rhode Island

Notes:
1. John H. Rhodes, *The History of Battery B, First Regiment Rhode Island Light Artillery* (Providence: Snow and Farnum, Printers, 1894) 370
2. Biographical Information compiled by Bruce Campbell MacGunnigle, May 24, 1992 courtesy of Battery B First Rhode Island Light Artillery Inc. Collection
3. *Find a Grave*, database and images (https://www.findagrave.com: accessed 25 October 2020), memorial page for George McGunigle (27 Aug 1845–21 Nov 1916), Find a Grave Memorial no. 131093132, citing Oak Grove Cemetery, Pawtucket, Providence County, Rhode Island, USA; Maintained by greenwich1677 (contributor 48706421)
4. George McGunigle Obituary. *Pawtucket Times,* November 21, 1916.
5. Naturalization Certificate belonging to McGunigle courtesy of Bruce MacGunnigle Collection
6. George McGunigle photos courtesy of Bruce MacGunnigle Collection
7. John Hickey photo courtesy of Battery B First Rhode Island Light Artillery Inc. Collection

GAMALIEL LYMAN DWIGHT

20

The Poet Soldier

Gamaliel Lyman Dwight was born on February 3, 1841, in Providence, Rhode Island. He was the son of Gamaliel Lyman and Catherine Henshaw (Jones) Dwight. As a boy, Dwight excelled in academics attending schools in Providence, Rhode Island. When the Civil War commenced in the spring of April 1861, Dwight was twenty- years-old and in his freshman year at Brown University. As the national conflict escalated, Dwight left his studies and enlisted on June 6, 1861, as a corporal with Battery A First Rhode Island Light Artillery. Tall, slender, and serious, Dwight would quickly rise through the ranks due to his intelligence, disciplined demeanor and, brave conduct during the war.

On November 29, 1861, Dwight would become a second lieutenant in Battery B First Rhode Island Light Artillery and later a first lieutenant in Battery A in November 1862. At Gettysburg, Dwight's horse would be shot out from underneath him but Dwight would remarkably escape serious injury. Despite the carnage and chaos of the war, Dwight took solace and relief in poetry and reading. He loved the works of John Stuart Mills and Sir William Hamilton. He carried their books and papers as part of his belongings during the many marches and campaigns of the war. Dwight also shared his love of reading and philosophy with his fellow soldiers. One cannoneer recounted, *"In a crowd, he disdained to talk much, but with a cup of chocolate by him, an open volume on his table, and a cigarette in his hand, he would discourse most marvelously on life, death and the mysteries of philosophy and psychology, until every voice would be hushed, but his own, and his auditors would listen with rapt attention, until the great wood fire, in which he luxuriated, died out, and the howling of the wind outside, or noise of distant picket firing, would bring us back to realize that we were not in the lecture room of a professor, but in the heart of the wilderness, surrounded by deadly enemies."* Such was the heart and soul of Dwight.

During his service in the war, Dwight wrote numerous heartfelt letters to his dear friend and fellow poet, Sarah Helena Whitman, who was also temporarily engaged to Edgar Allen Poe in December 1848. In Dwight's salutations, he refers to Sarah as Saint Helena. His letters read more like poetry than prose and are by far, some of the most eloquent letters among all the Battery B collection.

His April 29, 1862, letter begins, *"After a long lapse of time, your two fresh charming Spring letters, redolent of the violet and the Mayflower have blessed me."* He goes on to write, *"I am sorry you were unwell but hope that the inferior turn of life's wheel was but to gain fresh momentum..."* His letters to Whitman also tell the story of what it might have felt like to be in the artillery. With honesty and keen expression, Dwight conveys his innermost sentiments of battle. He writes, *"Should you linger a few minutes you could experience the poetry of being 'stormed at with shot and shell' to a nicety. I have taken laughing gas, alcohol and hash-sheesh and been frightened, but no experience compares with artillery practice. Here we have barracks and fortifications and men to fire at and when the ball opens with five hundred guns booming upon the air, it will be grand."* What is also striking about this letter is the particular way in which Dwight seems to bring Sarah directly into his physical experience. He is masterful at narrating exactly what is happening at the moment. He continues, *"I picked some violets for you the other day where a young lieutenant of infantry was shot yesterday, but they are quite faded now. (Note, a general with one arm just rode by, Very fine!)."*

Those that observed Dwight on the battlefield were amazed at his ability to remain calm under the most harrowing conditions. After the war, Lieutenant Colonel J. Albert Monroe of the First Rhode Island Light Artillery, described Dwight's demeanor during the First Battle of Bull Run. *"But the coolest one of our number, I believe, the coolest man on the field that day, was Sergeant G. Lyman Dwight. When the storm of bullets was thickest and the rebel artillery was delivering upon us its heaviest fire, Dwight would step aside from the smoke of his gun, and seemed perfectly absorbed by the sublime and magnificent spectacle…When the leaden rain and iron hail were thickest, I have known him to muse upon philosophy, and to repeat a quotation from some favorite author applicable to the situation and experience. He was quick and unerring, and no emergency could arise that would deprive him of his self-possession."*

When the war ended, Dwight returned home to his native Rhode Island and finished earning his degree from Brown University. He became a well-known physician and surgeon in Rhode Island. In January 1871, Dwight married Anne Ives Carrington. That same year, the newlyweds traveled to Europe where they had one daughter, Margarethe L. Dwight, born on November 8, 1871, in Berlin, Germany.

When the young family eventually returned to Providence, Rhode Island, Dwight's health began to fail and he was forced to abandon his medical practice. Dwight's doctors advised him to avoid the harsh Rhode Island winters and recommended he spend some time in a warmer climate. Acting on that advice, Gamaliel, Anne and, young Margarethe moved to Nassau in the Bahamas. Despite their attempt in moving to more hospitable weather, Dwight died on January 19, 1875. He was 33 years old. His wife and daughter had Dwight's body transported back to Rhode Island. He is buried at North Burial Ground in Providence, Rhode Island.

The legacy of Gamaliel Lyman Dwight lives on today through a scholarship at Brown University. In 1866, Gamaliel Lyman Dwight presented a scholarship fund to the University in honor of his grandfather, Judge David Howell, who was a member of the Continental Congress. Today, income from the David Howell Premium is awarded to students in their senior year who have the highest rank in math and natural philosophy.

Camp Winfield Scott:
Before Yorktown, Virginia.
Tuesday, 29 April, 1862.

My dear Saint:

After a long lapse of time your two fresh charming Spring letters, redolent of the violet and the May-flower, have blessed me. One dated the 11th, New York, came Saturday morning, and this morning at sunrise, — your sunrise, 11 o'clock, — came your other notelet from Providence. I am sorry you were unwell, but hope that the inferior turn of life's wheel was but to gain fresh momentum, and send you ad superiores astras.

At anyrate, but wait till June, and you and Helme and I will go up together, with Lester for ballast, to have the thing sure.

Surely, our arms have been crowned with victory of late, and it seems as if the rebellion only waited for Yorktown and Corinth for its end. The latter seems a sure victory. Yorktown is, too, if the rebels only stay, or show any kind of a fight. We are slowly getting ready, but when the drums beat, and the bugles cry, then stop every news boy, for extras will be extras, then. I could show you the rebels by a ten min utes' walk from camp, — their works and flaunting colors. Should you linger a few minutes, you could experience the poetry of being "stormed at with shot and shell" to a nicety. I have taken laughing gas, alcohol, hash-hash and been frightened, but no excitement compares with artillery practice. Here we have barracks and fortifications and men to fire at; and when the ball opens, with five hundred guns booming upon the air, it will be grand! I picked some violets for you the other day where a young lieutenant of infantry was shot yesterday, but they are quite faded now. (Note. A general with one arm just rode by. Very fine!) April Showers — forty-eight hours long — are very common now, and very disagreeable. Sprinkling now! How I would like to be with the three Saints once more! My love to Santa Anna and St. Mansfula; will write to the latter soon. Thank her for "The Major's Millions". I am glad Nora is more comfortably situated. Miss Anna's Address is teeming with good things, I know. What new costume has she devised recently? How complete her Zouave dress was!) How is Miss Lizzie Potter now, — and Mr and Mrs Whitaker? Placing implicit reliance in your prayers and the horse-shoe, I am

My regards to Helme and Williams and Shipley and Mrs Hart and all. Do you not often meet many Pleasant Dreams?

With love,
Ever Yours
Lyman.

Dwight's letter to his friend, Sarah Helena Whitman dated April 29, 1862

Grave of Gamaliel Lyman Dwight, North Burial Ground, Providence, Rhode Island

Notes:
1. John H. Rhodes, *The History of Battery B, First Regiment Rhode Island Light Artillery* (Providence: Snow and Farnum, Printers, 1894) 352
2. https://rhodeislandgenealogy.com/providence/biography-of-gamaliel-lyman-dwight-m-d.htm
3. https://bulletin.brown.edu/prizespremiumsandhonors/
4. http://www.ric.edu/northburialground/tours_civilwar-dwightgamaliel.html
5. Photo of Gamaliel Lyman Dwight courtesy of Leo Kennedy
6. Grave photo courtesy of Battery B First Rhode Island Light Artillery Inc. Collection
7. Albert J. Monroe, *Personal Narratives of the Battles of the Rebellion* (Providence: Sidney S. Rider, 1878) 17-19
8. Letters belonging to Gamaliel Lyman Dwight courtesy of Brandon Hall

JOSEPH STODDARD CASSEN

21

Not Once But Twice

Only a nightmare could have been more hideous, but this place was no nightmare. Private Joseph Stoddard Cassen closed his eyes and opened them, focusing on the horror he saw upon entering the camp. The first thing he discerned was the 15-foot-high stockade walls that surrounded the perimeter. Confederate guards eyed his every move. Cassen noticed the rope line that prison guards placed about 20 feet from the inside of the stockades. This he soon came to know as the "dead line," marking the restricted space that kept camp prisoners from approaching the walls. If anyone crossed the rope line, they would be summarily shot. There were prisoners everywhere he looked. The Andersonville Prison was bursting at the seams and could barely contain the now more than 40,000 starving and disease-ridden soldiers detained there. Cassen also certainly experienced the camp's lack of food, general hygiene and freshwater supply. As the days grew into weeks, Cassen watched as these horrifying conditions transformed once energetic and patriotic soldiers into emaciated skeletons, who were left to die in the mud and excrement that covered the ground. And then there was the mental torment, especially for Cassen who couldn't believe his misfortune.

For Joseph Cassen, this was the second time in a matter of a few months that the Confederate Army had taken him prisoner. The first time he had been captured was on July 2, 1863, at Gettysburg. In the chaos of the battle, as the Confederate infantry stormed Battery B's extended position on Cemetery Ridge, Cassen was the only Battery B cannoneer captured that day. All the other soldiers from his Battery were either killed or wounded or managed to take cover near a stone wall and shield themselves from further danger. Cassen was initially held by Confederate forces but was eventually paroled at City Point, Virginia a month later on August 2, 1863, and was able to rejoin the Battery. That might have been bad enough but, at the Battle of Bristoe Station in October 1863, after only having been back with the Battery for a few months, Cassen was again captured. This time, he was sent further south and eventually condemned to the Andersonville prisoner of war camp.

Despite being held as a prisoner for nearly 12 months, Cassen survived and was eventually freed in a mutual prisoner exchange on November 7, 1864, in Savannah, Georgia. Upon his release, he would serve two more months with Battery B before he was formally discharged from federal service on January 8, 1865. He had served with Battery B for the entire war; having been an original member enlisting on August 13, 1861. After the war, Cassen returned home to Providence, Rhode Island, and worked as a jeweler and a silversmith. In 1880, nearly 15 years after his discharge from Battery B, Cassen filed for a veteran's military pension. He remained close to the Battery throughout the rest of his life and served on the Executive Committee of the Battery B Veteran Association in 1914. He lived until the age of 90 years old and died on April 19, 1933. He is buried at the North Burial Ground in Providence, Rhode Island.

Joseph Stoddard Cassen, North Burial Ground, Providence, Rhode Island

Notes:
1. John H. Rhodes, *The History of Battery B, First Regiment Rhode Island Light Artillery* (Providence: Snow and Farnum, Printers, 1894) 362
2. http://www.ric.edu/northburialground/tours_civilwar-cassenjoseph.html
3. https://allthatsinteresting.com/andersonville-prison
4. *Find a Grave*, database and images (https://www.findagrave.com: accessed 25 October 2020), memorial page for Joseph Stoddard Cassen (unknown–19 Apr 1933), Find a Grave Memorial no. 12621338, citing North Burial Ground, Providence, Providence County, Rhode Island, USA; Photo by Jen Snoots
5. Photo of Cassen courtesy of Battery B First Rhode Island Light Artillery Inc. Collection

JOHN GARDNER HAZARD

22

"Rhode Island's Gallant Soldier"

For several days, the smell of freshly fallen timber and the sound of axes filled the air of the Virginia countryside. Soldiers, who were once loggers and lumbermen in their former civilian lives, were busy leveling the trees and forests around the Union Second Corps Headquarters in Culpepper, Virginia. The occupying Union Army had also commandeered William Nalle's sawmill just south of Mountain Run creek and were working the mill day and night sawing logs into joists and boards. Construction was underway of a large building with the floors and walls made of lumber while quartermaster departments furnished canvas sheets for the roof. On Friday, February 19, 1864, the building was finally complete and the work commenced to adorn the

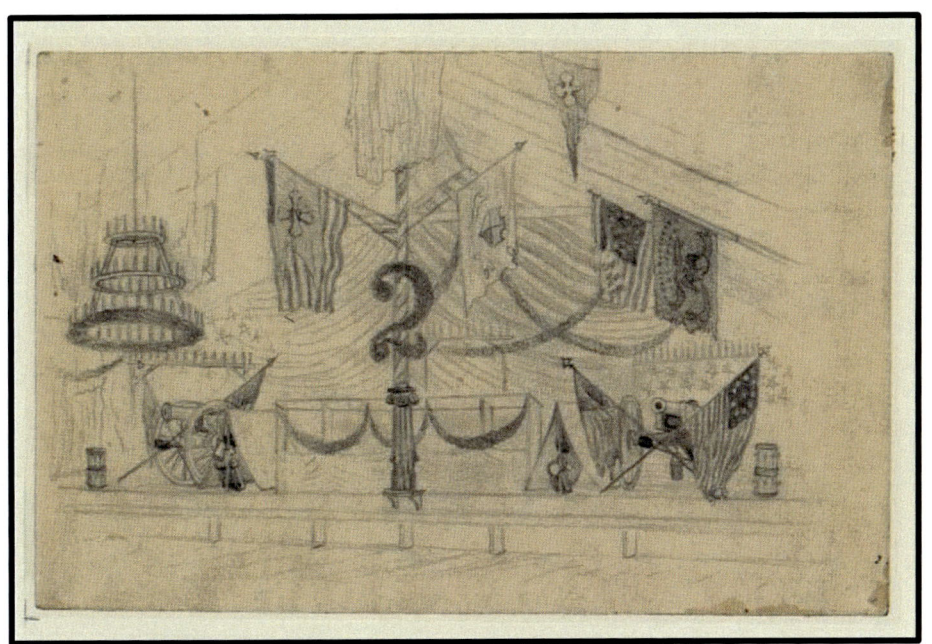

Stage with Battery B cannons, flags and two large mounted guns on post, by Edwin Forbes

interior of the wooden structure with red, white and, blue flags, banners, ribbons, and streamers that swayed from the timber rafters. On one end of the building was a raised platform. On each side of the platform sat two of the Battery's bronze light twelve-pounder artillery pieces. These cannons, adorned with flags and bunting, belonged to two of Battery B First Rhode Island Light Artillery's Sergeants, John Rhodes and Pardon

Walker who worked to meticulously position them in these places of high honor for the occasion.

On the evening of February 22, 1864, with all the painstaking preparations made, high ranking army officers and their guests began arriving at the newly constructed dance hall for a grand military ball in honor of George Washington's birthday. Ladies from Baltimore, Washington, Philadelphia, and even as far as New York, began to enter the beautifully decorated and impressively illuminated wooden ballroom. Among the distinguished attendees, that night were Senator William Sprague of Rhode Island and his beautiful wife, Katherine Jane Chase Sprague, who were the honored guests of Battery B First Rhode Island Light Artillery Captain, John Gardner Hazard.

John Gardner Hazard was born on April 15, 1832, in Exeter, Rhode Island to parents John and Margaret (Crandall) Hazard. As a young boy, he attended school in Rhode Island and worked as a merchant prior to the Civil War. During the summer of 1861, he enlisted as a regimental hospital steward. Two days later he became first lieutenant of Battery C on August 8, 1861. The 29-year-old officer played a significant role in the organization of Batteries B and C and was then transferred to Battery A on September 17, 1861. Hazard served bravely during the battles of Ball's Bluff, Yorktown and, Fair Oaks. On August 20, 1862, Hazard was commissioned Captain of Battery B First Rhode Island Light Artillery. When he finally took command on

Old mill on Mountain Run near Culpepper, by Edwin Forbes

September 1, 1862, the Battery was in bad condition. Horses and equipment needed to be replaced, and the men, tired from constant marching, had begun to relax discipline protocols. Hazard began immediately to implement the many needed improvements and completed them just in time.

Our Story

On October 1, 1862, the men of Battery B were buzzing with activity as they prepared for a special inspection. That afternoon, mounted on horseback, Captain Hazard had the honor of riding alongside President Lincoln and General McClellan as they went on a tour of inspection throughout the camp. Two months later in December 1862, Hazard would be on horseback again at the battle of Fredericksburg. Under murderous fire, Battery B had to race to its position on the field or risk being mowed down by the enemy fire. The battle was so intense that the Battery was only out on the field for forty-five minutes before sustaining multiple losses and had to be pulled back. General Couch later told the young Captain Hazard that he fully expected Battery B to be annihilated but considered the sacrifice necessary. During the battle, Hazard would have his horse shot and killed from underneath him. The young officer would survive Fredericksburg and in April 1863 he was commissioned Chief of the Artillery of the Second Corps. Four months later, Hazard was in charge of the Second Corps Artillery at the Battle of Gettysburg. Under his leadership, several batteries in his brigade unleashed a firestorm upon the Confederate artillery prior to Pickett's Charge. During the fierce cannonading, Hazard would once again have his horse shot out from underneath him. Less than a year later, in April 1864, Hazard was made a major of his regiment and fought through still more battles that year including the battles of Po River, North Anna, Cold Harbor, and eventually Petersburg. On August 8, 1864, he was made lieutenant colonel by brevet for 'gallant and meritorious services'. A year later, he was promoted again to Brigadier General for his outstanding service during the war. The highly decorated Hazard eventually mustered out of service on March 9, 1866. He was only 34 years old.

After the war, Hazard moved south and took up residence in the former Confederate State of Louisiana. He became a New Orleans cotton broker and commission merchant after his military retirement. He spent many years in the South running a successful business and traveling abroad.

On May 15, 1897, at the age of 65, General Hazard died in Providence, Rhode Island. Three days later, his body was carried into the Grace Episcopal Church in Providence, Rhode Island where funeral services were held in his honor. Mourners and friends filled the church on Westminster Street to pay their respects to the Civil War veteran who had given so much to Rhode Island's war effort. The Providence 'News', published that afternoon paid tribute to the General: *'The late John Gardiner Hazard, to whose memory the last tribute are to-day paid, was one of Rhode Island's gallant soldiers during the War of the Rebellion, and though his business career was made outside the home boundaries, he had a large acquaintance here and was greatly liked and esteemed in many circles. His sudden death was a shock to these many friends, for though the severe service of the soldier had undoubtedly had its effects on his physical constitution, he had all the spirit of young manhood, and was a charming associate wherever he moved.'*

General John Gardner Hazard is buried in Swan Point Cemetery, Providence, Rhode Island.

John G. Hazard headstone in Swan Point Cemetery, Providence, Rhode Island

Notes:
1. John H. Rhodes, *The History of Battery B, First Regiment Rhode Island Light Artillery* (Providence: Snow and Farnum, Printers, 1894) 126, 150, 183, 209, 214, 237, 265, 268, 271, 306,
2. Forbes, E. (1864) *Old mill on Mountain Run near Culpepper sic Court House, Va.* Culpeper Court House United States Virginia, 1864 [Photograph] Retrieved from the Library of Congress https://www.loc.gov/item/2004661548/
3. Forbes, E. (1864) Music Stand, 2nd Corps Ball, Camp Near Brandy Station Virginia, 1864 [Photograph] Retrieved from the Unites States Library of Congress, https://www.loc.gov/pictures/item/2004661860/
4. https://www.waymarking.com/waymarks/WMF5HT_Hazards_Brigade_US_Brigade_Tablet_Gettysburg_PA
5. The 'Providence News' Article, published May 18, 1897
6. http://sites.rootsweb.com/~rigenweb/articles/112.html
7. *Find a Grave*, database and images (https://www.findagrave.com: accessed 17 December 2020), memorial page for Gen John Gardner Hazard (15 Apr 1832-15 May 1897), Find a Grave Memorial no. 16217980, citing Swan Point Cemetery, Providence County, Rhode Island, USA, photo by Jen Snoots.
8. Photo of Hazard courtesy of Battery B First Rhode Island Light Artillery Inc. Collection

CHARLES H. BOWDEN

23

Son of Barrington Rhode Island

Charles H. Bowden was born in Providence, Rhode Island on February 5, 1846. As a child, he attended the public schools in Providence until the age of 18 when his family moved to Barrington, Rhode Island in the spring of 1864. That summer Bowden enlisted in Battery B First Rhode Island Light Artillery on August 24, 1864. He was with the Battery during the Siege of Petersburg in the final days of the war and received an honorable discharge on June 13, 1865.

When he returned home to Rhode Island, he married Sarah Eliza (Tiffany) Bowden on New Year's Day in 1867. They had one child, Helen Bowden, who was born on March 17, 1882. Both Charles and Sarah would outlive Helen who died at the age of 22 in 1904.

In 1913, Bowden joined several of his old Battery comrades at the 50th anniversary of the Battle of Gettysburg. During the celebration, Charles and several other cannoneers posed for a photo near Battery B's monument on the battlefield. As a devoted member of the Battery B Veteran Association, Bowden would serve as President from 1910-1911 and then again from 1917-1918. He would live until the age of 90 and passed away on September 22, 1936. Sarah would live to the age of 98 and die on October 10, 1942. Charles, Sarah and Helen are all buried together in Prince's Hill Burial Ground in Barrington, Rhode Island.

Of particular note, in 1826, Sarah's father, Ebenezer Tiffany, was appointed to lay out the design for the Prince's Hill Cemetery. He too was buried there upon his death in June 1864.

Tombstone of Charles, Sarah and Helen Bowden, Princes Hill Burial Ground, Barrington, Rhode Island

Notes:
1. John H. Rhodes, *The History of Battery B, First Regiment Rhode Island Light Artillery* (Providence: Snow and Farnum, Printers, 1894) 360
2. https://en.wikisource.org/wiki/A_History_of_Barrington,_Rhode_Island/Chapter_40
3. https://archive.org/stream/cu31924028840028/cu31924028840028_djvu.txt
4. *Find a Grave*, database and images (https://www.findagrave.com: accessed 25 October 2020), memorial page for Charles H. Bowden (5 Feb 1846–22 Sep 1936), Find a Grave Memorial no. 18040512, citing Princes Hill Burial Ground, Barrington, Bristol County, Rhode Island, USA; Maintained by Sons of Union Veterans of the Civil War (contributor 48353502).
5. Photo of Bowden courtesy of Battery B First Rhode Island Light Artillery Inc. Collection

JAMES MCGUNNIGLE

24

All Four Years

James McGunnigle was an original member of Battery B First Rhode Island Light Artillery enlisting on Tuesday, August 13, 1861. Born in 1841 in Nova Scotia, Canada, McGunnigle immigrated to America around the age of 11 when his mother, Mary McGunnigle, moved her five children to Providence, Rhode Island after the death of her husband, John McGunnigle.

When the Civil War began, James was nineteen years old. He originally enlisted in Company G, along with his younger brother, George McGunnigle, in mid-April 1861. Together, the two brothers fought in the First Battle of Bull Run. With his enlistment coming to a close in the summer of 1861, James McGunnigle decided to volunteer with Battery B First Rhode Island Light Artillery. He and his brother George would serve on Battery B's gun crews in several major battles including Ball's Bluff, Yorktown, Fair Oaks, and Malvern Hill. In September 1862, McGunnigle would be hospitalized due to sickness. He later would return to Battery B on March 28, 1863. At Gettysburg, James McGunnigle served on the Battery's third gun along with his brother, George McGunnigle, who was wounded during the intense fighting. In late July 1863, James McGunnigle would again receive treatment in the hospital and be reunited with the Battery in October of that same year. He would be officially mustered out of federal service on June 12, 1865. He served all four years during the civil war. Several years after he returned home, McGunnigle married Margaret Barry on March 18, 1872. They lived at 73 Point Street in Providence, Rhode Island where he worked as a feeder for the Providence Journal News, adding chemicals and solutions to equipment during the printing process. Together James and Margaret would have five children from 1872 through 1881. One son, named after his grandfather, John, died as an infant. Another son, named after his father, James, would later be committed to an asylum for setting fire to the Union Congregational Church's chapel in Providence, Rhode Island. McGunnigle's three other children: Elizabeth, William Henry, and Margaret would live into the 20th century, the youngest child lived until the year 1970. On July 2, 1884, the twenty-first anniversary of the battle at Gettysburg and the wounding of his brother George, James McGunnigle died, leaving his wife Margaret with three children under the age of eight years old. James McGunnigle was only 43 years old at the time of his death. He is buried at North Burial Ground in Providence, Rhode Island.

George McGunigle saw action at Gettysburg with his brother James.

James McGunnigle, North Burial Ground, Providence, Rhode Island

Notes:
1. John H. Rhodes, *The History of Battery B, First Regiment Rhode Island Light Artillery* (Providence: Snow and Farnum, Printers, 1894) 370
2. http://www.ric.edu/northburialground/tours_civilwar-mcgunniglejames.html
3. All photos of James McGunnigle courtesy of the Bruce MacGunnigle Collection

GIDEON SPENCER

25

"To Hell with Orders"

Two days before the Battle at Ream's Station, Virginia, on August 25, 1864, Gideon Spencer wrote home to his friend, George. *"My Captain is expecting to go home soon. I wish I was going in his place but never mind. I come this winter if I can."* That wish would not come to pass. Instead, Gideon would spend much of the winter as a prisoner of war.

Gideon Spencer was born in Warwick, Rhode Island on April 2, 1844. His parents, Thomas and Caroline (Remington) Spencer, invested in the young boy's education, enrolling him at the East Greenwich Academy and then Schofield Commercial College. In April 1861, at the outbreak of the war, Spencer was only seventeen years old. Despite not being of military age, he enlisted in Battery D First Rhode Island Light Artillery on September 4, 1861. Even as a young recruit, Spencer excelled as a soldier and was promoted quickly to the rank of sergeant. When his first term of enlistment was up, Spencer re-enlisted and was commissioned as a second lieutenant in Battery B First Rhode Island Light Artillery on April 26, 1864.

Over the next several months, Spencer would see fierce fighting with Battery B at places like Spotsylvania, North Anna, and Cold Harbor. In August 1864, Spencer would find himself at Ream's Station, Virginia. There, the Union Army forces had a singular mission: destroy the railroads. Though straightforward, this operation would be anything but easy. It's possible that Gideon Spencer saw some early signs that this engagement would not go as planned. One day before the march to Ream's Station, Spencer, under orders, hastily removed any identifying insignia from his and the Battery's caps and uniforms making it hard for the Confederate Army to identify the units of captured prisoners.

The march to Ream's Station was an arduous and exhausting experience. Spencer and his men marched through the night more than twelve miles to reach the front, removing fallen trees from the road purposely chopped down to prevent Union progress. On the morning of August 25th, without an hour of rest, Spencer and his two detachments of about fifteen men rolled the two artillery pieces into position. It was early morning, but, even in the growing light, Gideon knew there were problems with this position. The ground was muddy, making it hard to move the guns. The breastworks and makeshift trenches were too short and wouldn't afford the men much protection from incoming fire. It got worse. Gideon would look behind him to find a thirteen-foot-high mound made by a railroad cut, making any necessary escape a difficult task. But he wasn't able to contemplate these problems for long as rebel sharpshooters took aim and several men and horses fell dead.

Spencer immediately fired a couple of rounds in the direction of the deadly marksmen but was ordered to "ceasefire" as it was believed he was firing on Union soldiers. Incredulously, he obeyed orders but knew there must be some confusion about which men were across the field. There was no confusion, however, when sudden musket fire erupted from the nearby cornfields in front of Spencer's position.

Twenty Confederate artillery pieces opened up and shelled Battery B. Union lines began to break and Spencer and his gun crews were in trouble. With dozens of Confederate soldiers breaking through the lines, an officer shouted to Lt. Spencer: *"Why in the hell do you not fire upon the charging column?"* Spencer replied sharply that he was not able to fire a single shot

> Headquarters Battery HQ, B, 1st R.I. Lt. Arty
> Left of Petersburg, Va. August 22, 64
>
> Friend George,
>
> I have just received your kind letter this morning and was very glad to hear from you and that you answered so soon. I would like to make a trip to Newport R.I. I suppose I could take a trip to Newport Va. But that would not be such a nice visiting place as your Newport, R.I. is. So Lychi has got here.
>
> We have been down to Deep Bottom, out to the James River and up toward Richmond, but we did not take that little city. Last Saturday night we left there at dark. Marched all night; arrived at our new camp about ten o'clock in the morning through the mud for it had been raining two days and was still raining then, so we got quite wet. Besides the march yesterday morning we moved over to the left where we are now, expecting to march again soon. We had quite a fight here yesterday morning.
>
> My captain is expecting to go home soon. I wish I was going in his place but never mind. I come this winter if I can. Give my love to your mother and father and Miss Gorten if she has not gone home. And try to excuse this short letter for we are on the march now and when we get into camp again I will write a longer one. Please answer soon.
>
> Your friend,
> G. Spencer
>
> 2nd Lt. Batty B, 1st R.I. L.A.

Spencer Letter to his friend George, August 22, 1864

without firing upon the 10th Massachusetts Battery, whose position awkwardly jutted out in front of his location. To compensate, Spencer struggled to re-position his guns, now sinking into the soft mud, and aimed them at the advancing foe. It was a deadly storm of bullets and shells that caused considerable carnage. Nearly every Battery horse was killed and lay tangled in their harnesses. One of Gideon's men, Sergeant Calvin Macomber, was struck by a bullet. As his body recoiled from the blow, Spencer caught him before he hit the ground. Together with two other cannoneers, Spencer carried his bloodied comrade to the Union rear. Without fear for his life, Spencer raced back to the front and resumed command of his section. In that moment, a shell exploded and a piece of flying shrapnel cut one of Gideon's men completely in half from the waist down. The casualties continued. Gideon watched as Sergeant Adams was killed attempting to transport fresh supplies of ammunition. Lieutenant Perrin, who was in command of Battery B, took a piece of shell below the knee, shattering his shin. Men were falling fast. Gideon called for volunteers to help him service the Battery's guns. A few men heeded his call and fired what little was left in the limber chest. That's when Gideon noticed that an entire Union infantry unit in support of the Battery was not moving forward. Through the billowing smoke and groans of wounded men, Spencer shouted to the regiment's colonel to march his men into the fight. The colonel coolly replied that he had no orders to do so. *"To hell with orders,"* was Spencer's angry response, now almost completely depleted of men, ammunition, and horses. The colonel, however, would not move forward and eventually, the entire Union regiment, all 1,400 soldiers, including the colonel, would be taken prisoner without firing a single shot. Gideon continued to shell the enemy's positions using any available ammunition until only two of his fifteen men were left. It was hopeless. Spencer ordered the remaining Battery B cannoneers and federal soldiers who were by now exhausted and drained, to withdraw and make their way as best as possible to the Union rear. Lt. Spencer too, would try to do the same. But, as he carefully made his way up the steep embankment of the railroad cut, a solid shot from the enemy lines landed within feet of him. The sudden concussion of the blast threw Spencer into the air and slammed him hard to the ground. Shocked but unharmed, Spencer got to his feet and kept going. When he reached Halifax Road, he was surprised to see a familiar face in fellow comrade, Lieutenant Chace. Chace too, was ordered to fall back and was leading the only remaining Battery horse back to safety. As Spencer approached Chace in the road, a Confederate cannonball passed directly through the horse's body, instantly killing the animal. With nothing left to lose, Spencer and Chace made the brave decision to return to the Battery's position and attempt to fire the remaining canister rounds left in Chace's limber. They raced back down the embankment, but upon reaching their guns, were enveloped by fifty Confederate infantry soldiers, who took them prisoner.

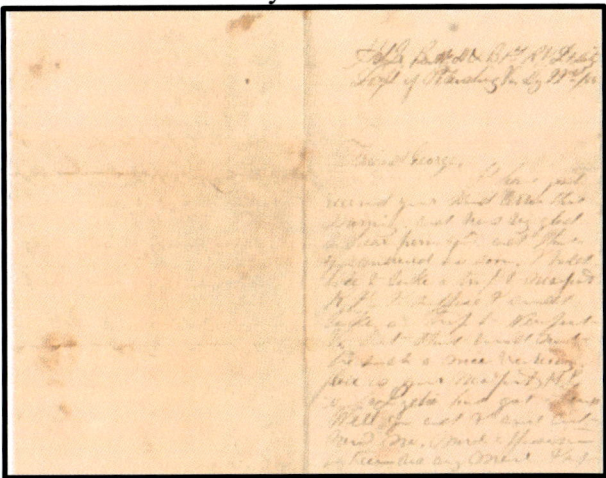

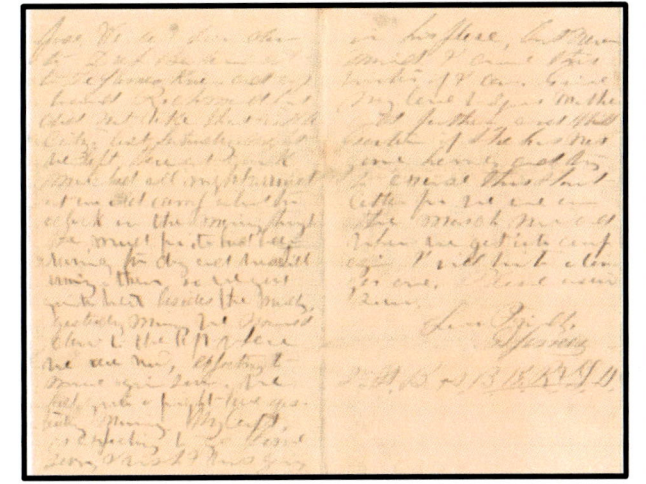

Gideon Spencer's Original Letter dated August 22, 1864

    Behind the enemy lines, Gideon noticed several Confederate soldiers dressed in Union uniforms, explaining the illusion earlier in the day of firing upon his own men. As Gideon observed this trickery with disbelief, he heard the distinctive blast of cannon fire coming from the Union lines. One of the remaining cannoneers from Battery B fired a parting shot, cutting a massive hole in the Confederate ranks now swarming the field. It would be midnight before the last of the remaining wounded soldiers both North and South would be dragged from the field. Fifty-two men of Battery B were killed, wounded, or captured. Another fifty horses were slaughtered. Four cannons and caissons were lost.

As a prisoner, Spencer was sent to the dreaded Libby Prison in Richmond, Virginia. The conditions in the four-story prisoner building were miserable but better compared to the deprivations that Spencer would face at Salisbury Prison. Deadly disease and diarrhea killed an estimated 4,000 weary prisoners. In November 1864, Spencer was transported to Danville Prison in West Virginia. There, other prisoners like Spencer endured horrible conditions. Spencer was confined to a three-story factory that had been converted into a prison. Food was scarce and disease was rampant. The cold temperatures were unbearable. Numerous prisoners died each day. Somehow, Spencer survived and was paroled in February 1865. He would return to his regiment and be promoted to 1st Lieutenant Battery F First Rhode Island Light Artillery. On June 27, 1865, at the age of 21, after more than three years at war, he would be mustered out of service and finally return home to Rhode Island, fulfilling his earlier promise to his friend George.

Gideon Spencer would go on to marry Martha Mathewson and spend the rest of his life in Warwick, Rhode Island. They had three children: Joseph, Henry, and Caroline (named after his mother). He studied dentistry and opened his practice on Westminster Street in Providence. He served on the Rhode Island Legislature and the Warwick School Committee for many years championing education and veteran soldiers. Spencer was instrumental in creating the Soldiers Home in Bristol Rhode Island and would later perform as the Soldier's Home's Secretary. Finally, he also served as Department Commander of the Rhode Island Grand Army of the Republic. On March 3, 1918, at the age of 74, Gideon Spencer died at his residence. Today, his body is interred at Swan Point Cemetery in Providence, Rhode Island.

Gideon Spencer Grave, Swan Point Cemetery, Providence, Rhode Island

Notes:
1. John H. Rhodes, *The History of Battery B, First Regiment Rhode Island Light Artillery (Providence: Snow and Farnum, Printers, 1894),* 96-98
2. *http://sites.rootsweb.com/~rigenweb/articles/162.html*
   History of the State of Rhode Island and Providence Plantations: Biographical
3. *https://www.ncpedia.org/confederate-prison-salisbury*, Louis A. Brown, 2006
4. *https://www.mycivilwar.com/pow/va-danville.html*, The American Civil War, Danville Prisoner of War Camp
5. *Find a Grave*, database and images (https://www.findagrave.com: accessed 27 October 2020), memorial page for Gideon Spencer (2 Apr 1844–3 Mar 1918), Find a Grave Memorial no. 26468392, citing Swan Point Cemetery, Providence, Providence County, Rhode Island, USA; Photo of Spencer grave courtesy of Carlo
6. Photo of Gideon Spencer courtesy of Battery B First Rhode Island Light Artillery Inc. Collection

GEORGE R. MATTESON
&
BENJAMIN W. MATTESON

26

Brothers

Jeremiah and Sally Matteson could have never guessed from their home in West Greenwich, Rhode Island, the carnage that was taking place on a muddy embankment in Virginia on Monday, October 21, 1861. That Monday, at the battle of Ball's Bluff, three of their sons, George, Benjamin and, William, were serving on Battery B First Rhode Island Light Artillery's only gun detachment in the battle. What started off as a small Union scouting expedition the day before, had turned into a full-scale engagement. By the end of the day, due to faulty intelligence and poor communication, the Union army would suffer a stinging defeat. As a result, Battery B and the three Matteson boys from Rhode Island would pay a heavy price.

In 1861, the patriarch of the Matteson family was 67-year-old Jeremiah Matteson from West Greenwich, Rhode Island. He and his wife Sally, who was 58 years old by the time of the Civil War, had nine children together. Their first child, David Andrew (named after his paternal grandfather), died before he turned one in 1825. Their second son, John Waterman, was born two years later, followed by their first and only daughter, Dorcas, in 1828. Their family kept growing and by 1832, they gave birth to their third son, William Matteson. Two years later, they would have another son, David, who also died before he would turn one year old. A year later, Benjamin was born in 1835, followed by George in 1837. Three years later, Edwin arrived followed by their last-child, Jeremiah (named after his father) who was born in 1843.

In August 1861, William, Benjamin, and George enlisted on the same day, August 13, 1861, with Battery B First Rhode Island Light Artillery in Providence, Rhode Island to serve with the Union Artillery. One year later, on August 13, 1862, Edwin Matteson, enlisted with Battery E First Rhode Island Light Artillery. In all, four sons from the same family left their home in West Greenwich, Rhode Island to join the Union cause.

In October 1861, roughly a couple of months after William, George, and Benjamin enlisted, they would see action at the battle of Ball's Bluff in Virginia. Preceding the engagement, fourteen men, seven horses, one cannon, and one limber of Battery B crossed the Potomac River into enemy territory in Virginia. When they arrived on the Virginia shore, they hauled the gun and limber, weighing nearly a ton, up a steep cliff and dragged it into position. Once the Battery was in place, they began shelling the enemy position. Confederate artillery and musketry took a heavy toll on Battery B. All seven horses were killed. The Battery's only cannon and limber were captured, and all but two of the Battery cannoneers were shot. Those that were not shot, like Merritt Tillinghast, plunged into the swollen Potomac River and swam for safety to the Maryland shore. He would eventually reach the riverbank a half-mile downstream from where he started and exhausted, rejoined the Battery the next day. As for those who were wounded, it was a different story. Weak and cold, the wounded men took cover as best they could behind an abandoned house and waited until dark. They used saddle blankets from the dead horses to care for those badly wounded. Eventually, the wounded were evacuated by fresh Union soldiers, across the river to receive medical attention at a hospital in Poolesville, Maryland.

William Matteson, the oldest of the brothers, was captured during the battle and taken prisoner. Missing and unable to send word of his whereabouts, his brothers thought he had drowned in the Potomac River as many other Union soldiers had during their hasty retreat. That was not the case though, and he would later be part of a prisoner exchange on May 28, 1862. He rejoined the Federal Army and stayed with Battery B until he mustered out of service on August 12, 1864.

Benjamin Matteson was shot through both legs just above the knees. He spent several months recovering from his wounds but was unable to serve in the artillery any longer. On August 21, 1862, he bade goodbye to his younger brother and was discharged home to Rhode Island. George Matteson had two mini balls miraculously pass through his hat and never touch a piece of hair. But that kind of good fortune would not hold out. Moments later, George felt a searing pain, as another mini ball entered his side and exited his back, just missing his spine. Wounded but alive, he would be hospitalized, recover, and return to Battery B. On September 7, 1862, he was promoted to lance corporal.

A year later, Corporal George Matteson and the men of Battery B would be hotly engaged at the battle of Gettysburg in July 1863. On that hot summer afternoon, Matteson took up his position as the number six man, whose function was to prepare the ammunition rounds to be fired and hand them to the number five man, who would provide them to the number two man of the field piece. At his post behind the Battery's limber chest, he would stand witness to the gruesome deaths of his comrades, Alfred Gardner and William Jones, who were killed when a rebel shell struck the muzzle of the cannon.

When the Battery was out of ammunition and ordered to the rear, the young twenty-six-year-old remained on the field. Mesmerized by the sea of gray uniforms that were advancing across the open pastures toward the Union position on Cemetery Hill, Matteson stayed to witness Pickett's Charge. That decision was a costly one. During the attack, George Matteson was wounded again and taken off the field to a Union field hospital behind the lines. Just as before, he would recover, and serve the remainder of the war, before being mustered out of service the same day as his brother, William, on August 12, 1864.

As for younger brother, Edwin Matteson, he would never come home. Four months after his enlistment with First Rhode Island Battery E, the nineteen-year-old Rhode Islander would die a few days before Christmas in a Falmouth, Virginia hospital from dysentery. He would become the third son lost to his aging parents, Jeremiah and Sally. William Matteson would go on to marry Amy Barber Matteson and have three children. He died in Coventry, Rhode Island on October 25, 1907, right around the 46th anniversary of his capture at Ball's Bluff. He is buried in Wood River Cemetery in Richmond, Rhode Island.

Benjamin Matteson would suffer from his leg wounds for the rest of his life. He married Delia Barber, and together they had one daughter, Buela Bell, who died when she was four months old on April 4, 1870. Benjamin died on May 29, 1915, at the age of 79. He is buried along with his wife in the David Matteson Lot in West Greenwich, Rhode Island. George Matteson would go on to marry Hannah Gallup Matteson. He died on April 19, 1920, at the age of 82, and is buried at Gallup Cemetery, Connecticut.

Tombstone of George Matteson, Gallup Cemetery, Connecticut

Benjamin Matteson, David Matteson Lot, West Greenwich, Rhode Island

William Matteson, Wood River Cemetery, Richmond, Rhode Island

Notes:
1. John H. Rhodes, *The History of Battery B, First Regiment Rhode Island Light Artillery* (Providence: Snow and Farnum, Printers, 1894) 33-46, 369
2. Straight, Albert Aaron. Letter to his brother John Straight. 2 November 1861. Courtesy of Battery B First Rhode Island Light Artillery, Inc. Collection
3. *Find a Grave,* database and images (https://findagrave.com:accessed 19 December 2020), memorial page for George Reynolds Matteson (1837-19 Apr 1920), Find a Grave Memorial no. 77613013, citing Gallup Cemetery, Sterling Windham County Connecticut, USA: Photo by Nate Bramlett.
4. *Find a Grave*, database and images (https://www.findagrave.com: accessed 19 December 2020), memorial page for William Francis Matteson (15 Mar 1832-25 Oct 1907), Find a Grave Memorial no.182956295, citing Wood River Cemetery, Richmond, Washington County, Rhode Island, USA, Maintained by Jonathan Laing (contributor 46564844).
5. *Find a Grave,* database and images (https://www.findagrave.com: accessed 19 December 2020), memorial page for Benjamin W. Matteson (13 Sep 1835–29 May 1915), Find a Grave Memorial no. 7338216, citing David Matteson Lot, West Greenwich, Kent County, Rhode Island, USA; Photo by Jonathan Laing.
6. Photo of Mattesons courtesy of Battery B First Rhode Island Light Artillery Inc. Collection

DAVID HENRY PHETTEPLACE

27

Father and Son

David Henry Phetteplace was born on January 26, 1846, in Smithfield, Rhode Island to parents David Phetteplace and Sarah Weldon Humes Phetteplace. At the young age of 15, David enlisted as a corporal with Battery B First Rhode Island Light Artillery on August 13, 1861, in Providence, Rhode Island. Enlisting alongside David Henry was his father, 41-year-old David Phetteplace, a native of Connecticut. Together both father and son served in every major engagement during the Civil War with Battery B. David Henry's brother, Lewis Trescott, also served during the conflict with the United States Signal Corps.

When the war was over, the elder Phetteplace remained in Rhode Island with his wife, Sarah. David Henry, the son, moved to Maryland shortly after being mustered out of service on June 12, 1865. On December 15, 1870, he married Elizabeth Masters, who in 1850, arrived in Baltimore with her parents aboard the ship "Goethe" from Germany. Together the young couple would have four children Louis, David, Lottie, and John. As a veteran and civilian, David Henry established himself as a prominent fruit grower and was active as the superintendent of the Sunday School of the Reformed Church in Cavetown, Maryland, where he served for 14 years.

Both David Henry and Elizabeth would experience tragedies as a family. In 1874, Elizabeth's brother, Martin, was struck by a train and later died from his injuries. In 1896, Lewis Trescott Phetteplace, David's brother, would also die at a young age. On February 21, 1921, Elizabeth suffered a stroke and passed away at the age of 72. Seven weeks later her grieving husband, David Henry, died at their home at 8:15 in the morning from heart failure. He was 76 years old. Both David Henry and Elizabeth are buried in the Mausoleum in Rose Hill Cemetery in Hagerstown, Maryland.

David Phetteplace, David Henry's father, would lose his sight and eventually spend his final days at the Soldier's Home in Bristol, Rhode Island. He died on April 7, 1907, at the age of 87. He is buried at North Burial Ground in Bristol, Rhode Island.

David Henry Phetteplace Mausoleum in Rose Hill Cemetery in Hagerstown, Maryland

David Phetteplace tombstone at North Burial Ground, Bristol, Rhode Island

Notes:
1. John H. Rhodes, *The History of Battery B, First Regiment Rhode Island Light Artillery* (Providence: Snow and Farnum, Printers, 1894) 371
2. David Henry Phetteplace Obituary. *The Daily Mail*, March 28, 1921, Page 8, Column 1
3. Photos of David Henry Phetteplace and graves courtesy of Battery B First Rhode Island Light Artillery Inc. Collection

JOHN DELEVAN

28

The Historian

His hand stretched out and touched the massive 4 ½-ton seven-foot-high granite monument bearing the name, *"Brown's Battery."* The square pillar, dedicated to Battery B First Rhode Island Light Artillery, had been erected on the very ground the Battery occupied on July 3, 1863. His eyes glanced at the round cannonball that topped the monument mined from Westerly, Rhode Island. His eyes glistened in the cool autumn air as the trees of the Gettysburg countryside changed colors. He looked out over the rolling pastures of the Nicholas Codori Farm bedecked with small wildflowers and became overwhelmed with emotion.

It was Wednesday, October 13, 1886, and 45-year-old John Delevan was asked to make the dedication remarks at the newly placed Battery B monument. Somberly, his words sliced into the morning silence. *"I feel more like sitting down and bowing my head and letting memory take its sway at this time and place, than in attempting to speak,"* he began. His words brought forth a wave of emotion as he continued his remarks recounting the three days that the men of Battery B struggled and died on that very ground where he now stood. Delevan spoke of his slain comrades, *"torn, mangled, bleeding, dying in the full vigor of manhood and health...O! Cruel, cruel, war."*

Indeed, it was a cruel and terrifying battle. Delevan and the gun crews of Battery B were in a critical position on the field. They could see the Confederate soldiers reloading on their left flank; their caps pulled tightly around their eyes. It was July 2, 1863, on Cemetery Ridge at Gettysburg. Battery B cannoneers were in the process of trying to remove their guns from the field to allow the Union infantry to fire upon the rebel assault now rolling across the high grass. *"For God's sake, get this gun out of here quick,"* shouted a young soldier from the Fifteenth Massachusetts. As Delevan and another sergeant strategized as to how to remove their guns, a shot struck the officer, dropping him to the ground.

Delevan shouted to the drivers to bring up the horse teams and hitch the guns. But in the confusion of the battle, the drivers were only able to successfully haul four guns to safety. Delevan, in despair, threw himself down near one of the abandoned guns and waited for his fate. The Confederate infantry rolled up on Delevan's precarious position. As they approached, the young soldier from the Fifteenth Massachusetts, who had tried to help Delevan, was shot dead. Delevan looked ahead and behind him. He was caught midway between Confederate infantry and the Union infantry with their rifles leveled across the stone wall. A sheet of fire erupted from the Union soldiers and Delevan thought for certain he would be killed. His life flashed before his eyes.

That young life started 22 years earlier when John Delevan was born in Lowell, Massachusetts on May 20, 1841. At the outbreak of the national conflict, the young man enlisted as an original member of Battery B on August 13, 1861, in Providence, Rhode Island. He had been with Battery B for almost two years before that hot afternoon at Gettysburg and was prepared to accept his fate and die on the battlefield as a good soldier would.

It was then that he saw it, a hole in the ground about ten yards across and about two yards from the stone wall. Delevan dove into the hole as the smoke from the musket fire burned his eyes. As he slowly raised his head, he noticed there was another artillerist from Battery B already in the ditch. The cannoneer smiled at Delevan and then covered his head again as both sides exchanged volleys. As the fight raged on, the 69th Pennsylvania joined the battle and with their added support, the enemy fire ceased. He lingered a couple of moments and then Delevan jumped up and dashed for the cover of the stone wall. Two Union soldiers trained their rifles in his immediate direction as if he were a Confederate skirmisher. The two Union soldiers released their deadly shots but, they whizzed by Delevan striking two rebels who were trying to retreat. Breathing a sigh of relief, Delevan raced to catch up with Battery B, who had given him up for dead and appointed his good friend, William Jones, to take his place in the position as a gunner. Both men were quite happy to see each other after such an ordeal.

That night Delevan, tired and hungry, could hear the groans of the dying soldiers who seemed to be everywhere on the field. In the light of the almost full moon, he went out with several men to unharness some of the dead horses where they fell during the battle. The next morning dawned hot, humid, and quiet. Delevan tried to sleep amidst the clattering of canteens and wafting smoke of tobacco pipes. At 1:00 in the afternoon, he felt the ground shake underneath him and he then saw a shell burst overhead. Disoriented and trying to get his bearings, the young soldier ran to the front where artillery pieces were lined up in battle formation. As he ran up to the Battery's position, a piece of shell struck him in the left shoulder.

Though wounded, Delevan picked himself off the ground and kept moving. He witnessed horses, with their inwards dragging on the grass and explosions that were sending men into the air, blowing them apart. Reaching his field piece, he joined his friend, William Jones, and began cutting fuses as part of the detachment of the fourth cannon. To his left, he realized the third gun was without a gunner and so he ran over to that gun to fill the critical role. At that same moment, William Jones relieved a fellow gunner on the fourth piece as the shelling continued. Within seconds, a massive explosion occurred when a Confederate shell hit the muzzle of the fourth gun instantly killing William Jones and mortally wounding Alfred Gardner. Though the remaining officers tried to reload the gun, the muzzle was too badly damaged and the Battery was ordered to limber to the rear. Delevan however, was too weak to move and could barely walk. He crumpled to the ground as the men began to pull the remaining guns out of the way as the relief batteries took their place. He laid on the ground as the Union infantry sprang up from their posts ready to receive the gray wave of 14,000 Confederate soldiers advancing toward the Union Line atop Cemetery Ridge. Knowing the hardship of being trapped the day before, John Delevan mustered all his strength and hurried to rejoin the Battery survivors behind the Union lines. He would go on to fight the rest of the war serving with Battery B until Lee's surrender at Appomattox Court House in 1865. When John returned home after his service with Battery B, he found employment as a machinist working in Woonsocket, Rhode Island. On what would be the eighth-year anniversary of his experience at Gettysburg, Delevan married Eliza D. Kingsley on July 2, 1871. They had two children, who sadly both died at a young age. The Delevan's lived in Woonsocket, RI for about 25 years before moving to Westerly, Rhode Island, where John Delevan worked for Cotrell's press works. Later took up employment as a mail carrier and superintendent of mail carriers in Westerly, Rhode Island. On August 13, 1880, Delevan was elected President of the Battery B Veteran Association and was appointed historian and chair of a special committee to record the history of Battery B. For years, he implored surviving members to provide recollections, data, and information to compile the regimental history. Delevan was responsible for initiating the Battery history that John Rhodes eventually took up and completed. In 1886, John Delevan traveled to Gettysburg, Pennsylvania as part of the dedication committee to consecrate the monument dedicated to Battery B's service during the battle.

Battery B Monument at Gettysburg

At Gettysburg on that October morning in 1886, John spoke of the gratitude for the service of those who struggled and died on that ground. He said, *"I feel that we the survivors have much to be thankful for...As I stand on this sacred spot, I cannot help comparing the occasion of this visit with that of our first visit so many years ago. We have a duty to perform today...we are here to dedicate this monument, sacred to the memory of our unfortunate and revered comrades who fell at this place, dying in the full vigor of manhood."* His service and experience during the battle at Gettysburg and his service throughout the war forever shaped him as a soldier, a veteran, and a civilian. In 1907, Delevan was employed as an elevator operator at the Longley Building in Woonsocket, Rhode Island. On January 30, 1909, as he made his way to work that cold morning, he suffered a massive heart attack. Bystanders saw Delevan collapse to the ground. They carried his lifeless body into a nearby grocery store where he was pronounced dead. His funeral service was held at his home at 426 Grove Street, Westerly, Rhode Island. He is buried at River Bend Cemetery, Westerly, Rhode Island.

John Delevan tombstone, River Bend Cemetery, Westerly, Rhode Island

Notes:
1. John H. Rhodes, *The History of Battery B, First Regiment Rhode Island Light Artillery* (Providence: Snow and Farnum, Printers, 1894) 357, 395-399
2. Delevan, John. A Presentation at Gettysburg, July 2&3 1863. Courtesy of Battery B First Rhode Island Light Artillery Inc. Collection
3. Delevan, John. Letter to Charles Tillinghast Straight, 30 December 1906. Courtesy of Battery B First Rhode Island Light Artillery Inc. Collection
4. *Find a Grave*, database and images (https://www.findagrave.com: accessed 29 October 2020), memorial page for John Delevan (1841–1909), Find a Grave Memorial no.14908587, citing River Bend Cemetery, Westerly, Washington County, Rhode Island, USA; Maintained by Sherry (contributor 46802479)
5. All other photos courtesy of Battery B First Rhode Island Light Artillery Inc. Collection

CALEB H.H. GREENE

29

"A Perfect Hornet's Nest"

Caleb H.H. Greene was twenty-one years old when he mustered into service with Battery B First Rhode Island Light Artillery on October 5, 1861. The young farm laborer from West Greenwich, Rhode Island would spend a little more than a year with the Battery before being badly wounded at the Battle of Fredericksburg in December 1862.

Greene was one of sixteen men who was severely wounded within a span of forty-five minutes on the battlefield that cold December day. The Battery B cannoneers took mini balls and spent shell fragments in the hip, feet, wrists, neck, and groin. Twelve horses were killed in that same short span of time. John H. Rhodes, who later authored the Battery B Regimental History, narrated, *"Our position was a perfect hornet's nest, with the hornets all stirred up. Mini balls were flying and singing about us, with a zip and au-u-u or a thud as they struck; though they flew thick and fast we were too busy to dodge them, but kept our guns blazing away much to the consternation of those in front of us."*

During the ferocious battle at Fredericksburg, a Battery B soldier or horse was wounded or killed roughly every two minutes while out on the field. The Battery was purposely meant *"to be sacrificed if need be, in order to give inspiration to the infantry in the last and great struggle of our troops to carry the works of the enemy at the stone wall,"* reported Rhodes in the Battery B Regimental History. Caleb Greene was one of those young men who was sacrificed. When the Battery was finally pulled off the field, Greene was carried to a nearby triage station and then taken to a Union hospital in Washington, DC. On October 9, 1863, he was transferred to the Veteran Reserve Corps, which was established for Union soldiers who could no longer serve on the field but, could perform light work, guard prisoners, and perform the duties of a clerk. After a year of serving with the reserve, Greene was formally discharged on October 24, 1864. Only two months after he returned home to his native Rhode Island, Greene died on his 24th birthday, Christmas Day 1864. He is buried in Benjamin Greene Lot, West Greenwich, Rhode Island.

Headstone belonging to Caleb H.H. Greene, West Greenwich, Rhode Island

Notes:
1. John H. Rhodes, *The History of Battery B, First Regiment Rhode Island Light Artillery* (Providence: Snow and Farnum, Printers, 1894) 140-144, 365
2. Photo of Greene and Greene Headstone courtesy of Battery B First Rhode Island Light Artillery Inc. Collection

**JAMES BLADE
(ALIAS JAMES MALANEY)**

30

One Soldier, Three Enlistments

The early morning sun streamed through the stained-glass windows of Saint Joseph's Catholic Church in Natick, Rhode Island. Family and friends of the deceased, James Blade, including his nine children and sixteen grandchildren, lined the wooden pews to say farewell to the man they had known their whole lives. But the man they knew as father and grandfather was also a soldier and sailor, though he never talked about that part of his life. He was quiet and reserved. He kept the horrors of the Civil War and the things he experienced to himself.

James Blade was born in Manchester, England on January 5, 1842. He and his family immigrated to America when he was 14 years old and settled in Rhode Island in 1856. In May 1862, as the war was entering its second year, the young, blue-eyed, 5'6" tall Blade, enlisted in the 9th Rhode Island Volunteers and served with that unit until September 1862, when the group disbanded. In 1863, he joined the Union Navy and served as a landsman in the Potomac Flotilla on the steam tug, *USS Yankee*. On August 2, 1864, Blade enlisted in the United States Army as a corporal in Battery A First Rhode Island Light Artillery under the alias of James Malany. He then became a member of Battery B First Rhode Island Light Artillery when Battery A merged with Battery B on September 23, 1864. A year later on June 12, 1865, Blade mustered out of service and returned home to Rhode Island.

Not long after he returned home from military service, James Blade married a young Ireland native, Catherine Whalen Blade. Together they built a family and raised three sons and six daughters. He worked as a carriage maker on Union Street in Providence and eventually bought the workshop where he had worked for more than 35 years.

In 1926, his wife Catherine would pass away leaving James a widower for twelve years before he too, would succumb to a long illness. He died on Tuesday, February 8, 1938 at 96 years old. Three days later, his large family formed the funeral cortege that lined Providence Street outside of Saint Joseph's Church in West Warwick. When the high mass of requiem was finished at 10:00 that Friday morning, his body was taken to Saint Mary's Cemetery in West Warwick, Rhode Island. Blade lies there in repose today with his wife, Catherine.

Fellow Carriage Makers around 1900 from left to right: John Doyle, Smith Tabor, James H. Blade (son), Corporal James Blade (Battery B)

Home belonging to James Blade, Rhode Island

*James Blade burial site at Saint Mary's Cemetery,
West Warwick, Rhode Island*

Notes:
1. John H. Rhodes, *The History of Battery B, First Regiment Rhode Island Light Artillery* (Providence: Snow and Farnum, Printers, 1894) 358
2. http://www.navsource.org/archives/09/86/86077.htm
3. Newspaper articles from Battery B First Rhode Island Inc Collection
4. Fold3Naval Records for Enlistments at Philadelphia 1863
   https://www.fold3.com/image/284434953?rec=268447276
5. All photos courtesy of Battery B First Rhode Island Light Artillery Inc. Collection

ROBERT ALEXANDER LAIRD

31

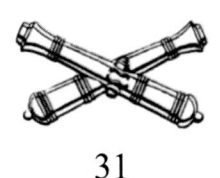

"Good to Die By"

As Robert Alexander Laird approached the small wooden podium to address the Grand Army of the Republic's Farragut Post in Riverside, Rhode Island, he paused for a moment to collect his thoughts. He was in the twilight of his life and his mind was awash with memories from the distant past. As he looked down, he could see his hands trembling ever so slightly as they grasped the edges of the old lectern. He stared at his hands for a brief second. Those hands he thought, now old and tired, had experienced so much. All his life, his hands had served him well, both in war and in peace, with only one exception. He tried hard to push that one memory back into the recesses of his mind as the audience looked up at him in anticipation. Though they had come to hear him speak about his experience during the war, it was his hands that told the real story of his service and his life.

Robert Laird was born in Belfast on February 14, 1840. He was born the fourth of five children to parents, Gilbert Galbraith Laird and Harriet Lovegrove Laird. Though hard-working, Gilbert and Harriet struggled to provide for their young family as the potato famine destroyed crops and lives across Ireland. In 1850, his parents and brothers and sisters, William, Catherine, Annie, and Thomas boarded a ship destined for the United States to seek a better life. The Laird family initially lived in New Jersey for a short time and then moved to Savannah, Georgia. Shortly before the Civil War erupted in 1861, Robert's family moved north to Rhode Island. Thomas Laird, the youngest of the family, however, remained in Georgia.

When the war broke out, Robert Laird and his brothers quickly enlisted in the war effort, but on opposite sides of the conflict. Robert Laird, who had labored with his hands as a machinist, left his job and enlisted as one of the original members of Battery B First Rhode Island Light Artillery on August 13, 1861, at the Benefit Street Arsenal in Providence. His older brother, William Laird, also enlisted in the Union, serving in the Navy. But, his younger brother, Thomas Laird, enlisted in the Confederate Army as part of the Montgomery Guards in Savannah.

Robert Laird saw constant action throughout the war at Ball's Bluff, Yorktown, Fair Oaks, Malvern Hill, Antietam, First Fredericksburg, Second Fredericksburg, Gettysburg, Bristoe Station, Mine Run, Wilderness, Po River, Spotsylvania, North Anna, Tolopotomoy, Cold Harbor and, Petersburg. Laird excelled as a soldier and was promoted on Sunday, December 15, 1861, as a corporal.

At the Battle of Gettysburg, Laird served in the right section, first gun, under Lieutenant William Perrin alongside Henry Hosea Ballou, Stillman Budlong, and

Mary Steele Laird

Private Albert Whipple. During the ensuing battle and ferocious fighting, Laird was standing at his position behind the limber chest when he was wounded in the hand, losing fingers in the process. Despite his gruesome and painful mutilation, Battery records do not indicate he ever left on a medical furlough. He was treated and continued to serve through 1864 when he was eventually and honorably discharged after his three-year enlistment was over on August 12, 1864. Laird returned home to Rhode Island and on March 7, 1866, he married Mary Steele. Mary was a young, attractive, and charming red-haired woman who also immigrated from Belfast, Ireland. Together they would raise nine children and were completely dedicated to each other. Mary loved Robert for his gentle and kind ways. She admired his deep love of history and literature. She also understood the deep pride he felt in having served in Battery B. In return, Robert showed his love for his wife and family by working hard to support them. After the war, he worked as a blacksmith, a trade he developed during his time with the Battery. Robert often mused about Mary's beautiful red hair. She was stoic, strict, and hardworking. To help provide for their nine children, Mary opened her own general store. Though firm at home, she was generous with her many patrons, giving goods and necessities away to those who needed assistance the most. Together, they lived a life of service, scrupulous honesty and extreme generosity that they hoped would serve as an example to their children. The family was everything to Robert and Mary. In the evenings after work, Robert would sit at his melodeon, his fingers dancing across the keys, playing songs he remembered during the war. Despite missing fingers, he never missed the opportunity to spend time with his family, with one exception.

It was that exception that kept creeping back into his mind as he readied himself to deliver his remarks to the Grand Army of the Republic. He finally let the memory unfold, cascading in small waves. He saw the scene in his mind just as it had happened many years ago. He was standing on the platform of the Providence Train Station awaiting the arrival of his brother. He had not seen his youngest brother, Thomas, since the family left Georgia. In the intervening years, Thomas Laird fought for the Confederacy, was taken prisoner and held at a Union prisoner of war camp, and, eventually released. Robert observed as the train pulled into the station.

He watched as his younger brother descended the train stairs and stepped onto the train's wooden platform. For a brief moment, Robert stared long at the younger brother he used to know and love but, somehow could not relate to anymore. He thought hard about extending his injured right hand in a handshake but ultimately, could not will himself to do it. Instead, he turned and walked away leaving Thomas on the platform before he was able to utter a single a word. The silence between the two brothers who fought on opposite sides of the conflict lasted longer than just that afternoon. The northern and southern sides of the Laird family would not make contact again and an eventual peace, until 1990. In 1913, Robert Laird attended the 50th Anniversary of Gettysburg and visited the hard-fought ground where he and others were wounded on Cemetery Ridge.

During the multi-day event, he experienced a change of heart. On the morning of July 2nd, Robert made the tough decision to wander into the Confederate camps in the hopes of finally finding his brother, Thomas. Despite his extended and desperate search among the Confederate veterans, he could not find him. The two brothers would never meet again.

Robert Laird taken in 1911 after a Memorial Parade in which he served as marshal. He is pictured here with his grandchildren: Robert Fournier, Stephen Nichols and William Laird.

Still, Robert's conviction for his service and the war remained strong his entire life. He served as the officer of the day for the Farragut Post for 36 years. Shortly before his death on March 7, 1922, he delivered a speech to his comrades, friends, and family at the Farragut Post in Riverside, Rhode Island. In his thick Irish accent, he delivered the following oration: "*I am here as a Grand Army man to represent Farragut Post. And I would say that I am not much of a talker and my education was mostly that which I got in the Army of the Potomac. This may seem peculiar to you children that a soldier should learn anything but what pertains to a battle or to fighting. However, I did learn to write and to learn many other things that made me better than I was. Before I had not the advantage of going to school as a great many had, but I done the best I could. When I left Providence in August 1861 to go to the front when Abraham Lincoln called for men to serve for three years or during the war, I enlisted in Battery B, the First Rhode Island Light Artillery for three years and I am proud to say today that I served the three years and was honorably discharged. In my Army life I have seen many curious and strange events. I did not dream what was before me. I did not realize the cruelty of war, but there was bright spots in my Army life I am glad to say. I hope the boys I see here today will always have a love for the stars and stripes—the dear old flag. It is good to die by—good to live by. But I hope you will never be called to defend your country's flag, for war is cruel. And I want to here say that in the Civil War, the men did not do it all. We had women, who if they did not carry a gun, done every in their power to help."*

Robert Laird is laid to rest at the Ancient Little Neck Cemetery in East Providence, Rhode Island. He was 82 years.

Tombstone of Robert Laird, Ancient Little Neck Cemetery, East Providence, Rhode Island

Notes:
1. John H. Rhodes, *The History of Battery B, First Regiment Rhode Island Light Artillery* (Providence: Snow and Farnum, Printers, 1894) 368
2. Laird, Robert. Letters, photos and speech text to Farragut Post. Courtesy of the Barbara Laird Collection, Exeter, Rhode Island.
3. Photos of Robert and Mary Laird courtesy of Barbara Laird Collection, Exeter, Rhode Island.

ALBERT AARON STRAIGHT

32

"No Sacrifices Too Great"

His hands were weaker now, shaking gently as he rubbed them together in an attempt to escape the chill of the room. His fingertips were pale where the dying sunlight caught them, not ghostlike, just subdued and grayish. His eyelids were heavy and his dark brown eyes were hollowed from fatigue and poor nutrition. The 32-year-old, 5'5" tall Union cannoneer couldn't sit up and so, gradually succumbed to the only position he could tolerate, lying down. His stomach pain came in waves and made him lurch and stiffen as the pain rose from his abdomen to his chest causing stomach acid to burn his throat. He gazed up at the ceiling and noticed the shadows slowly falling across the small hospital room.

It was November 15, 1863, and he had been there now for more than a month, confined to Ward A of the Fairfax Seminary Hospital in Alexandria, Virginia. He had been taken there by a long and painful ambulance ride, after initially being treated at the 2nd Corps Hospital in Culpepper, Virginia. It was in Culpepper, more than a month ago, in early October 1863, that he last saw his comrades from Battery B First Rhode Island Light Artillery. That day, Sergeant Albert Straight waved to his men as Battery B crossed the 2nd Corps hospital grounds on their way back to camp that fall. When they caught a glimpse of him, the men lifted their blue hats and gave him three exuberant cheers as they marched by.

That moment seemed like a long time ago. It was November now, high autumn, and Straight felt no improvement in his health. In fact, he was weaker now than when he had arrived at the Seminary Hospital on October 9, 1863. Time seemed to slow down as the days turned to weeks confined to his small cot. He rarely sat up anymore except when the nurses changed his sheets. He took those opportunities to look out the small window by his bed. He noticed that the leaves were already off the trees. Soon those fallen leaves would be beaten flat by the thousands of soldiers who would trample over them in the heavy rains and the first fall of snow as they went into winter camp. He wondered if he would ever rejoin them again. As he looked out upon the bare skeletal trees of the Virginia countryside, he couldn't help but think of himself, his body slowly being reduced to a skeleton from chronic diarrhea.

That condition had haunted him since December 1861 and now, had a full grip on his being. He was tired of being tired and tired of being sick. The medicines the doctors had been giving him, quinine, mercury with chalk, and opium, seemed to have little effect. His appetite was non-existent, and he refused the diet offered to

Fairfax Seminary Hospital, outside of Alexandria, Virginia (Library of Congress)

those who suffered from dysentery and diarrhea: tea and toast twice a day and beefsteak and potatoes for dinner.

There was no way he could eat, not with the feeling of fullness that he felt in his abdomen. Then there was the pain that seemed to wander from muscle to muscle without warning. He could feel his glands large and inflamed. He wondered how it had all come to this. In the waning daylight hours, his mind struggled to process just how vulnerable he was and how much of a toll his sickness had taken on him. He gently tilted his head back and closed his eyes letting his thoughts turn again and again to the events of the last three years.

He remembered that July afternoon in 1861 while visiting Quidnick, Rhode Island. It was there that he witnessed for the first time, the return of several soldiers from the First Rhode Island Regiment. That night he wrote to a friend. *"I have sometimes almost come to the conclusion that it is my duty to go and help sustain the Government of my Country. I think it is the duty of people to go, and have tried to look upon it from all points. It would be like parting life to leave, but I feel there are no sacrifices too great for one's country. I value my life but little, though would be pleased to see those little ones grow up and be trained in the way they should go, but feel to put my trust in a higher power, and give myself no trouble for this body, if I am but acting the part I should."* His life had been drastically altered by the time he saw those troops come home that summer day. Five years earlier, at the age of twenty-six, he married Angeline Avery Tillinghast Straight on February 24, 1856. That freezing winter day, the Reverend John Tillinghast, Angeline's father, married the young bride and groom in the presence of their family and friends at the Plain Meeting House in West Greenwich. Reverend John Tillinghast served as the pastor of the church and his new son-in-law, Albert, would serve as one of the deacons.

Albert and Angeline would take up residence in a small wooden house in West Greenwich, Rhode Island built almost 80 years before in 1783. On Wednesday, December 1, 1858, Angeline would give birth to their daughter, Laura Amanda Straight. Less than two years later, Charles Tillinghast Straight was born on October 27,

The Straight Homestead and birthplace of Laura Amanda Straight and Charles Tillinghast Straight, West Greenwich, Rhode Island

1860. Within a week, disaster would strike this small family. Exactly seven days after giving birth to her son Charlie, twenty-five-year-old Angeline died as a result of complications from childbirth on November 3, 1860. Both the Tillinghast and Straight families were devastated. With an infant in his arms and a two-year old by his feet, Albert Straight laid his young wife to rest in the Plain Meeting House Cemetery next to the church. Her grieving father presided at the funeral. Albert Straight struggled to pick up the pieces as a widower. For several months after his wife's death, he worked his farm and raised his two-year-old daughter and infant son, Charlie. But by July 1861, nearly nine months after burying his dear Angeline, he felt a strong pull to serve his country and the Union cause. Though initially torn between patriotism and paternal bonds, he would eventually enlist from West Greenwich on September 27, 1861, and be formally sworn into federal service on October 2, 1861, with Battery B First Rhode Island Light Artillery. Before leaving for Washington, DC on the steamer, *Kill Van Kull,* he entrusted the care of his dear children to his immediate family.

His three-year-old daughter, Laura, was sent by her father to live with her paternal grandmother and grandfather, Aaron and Abigail Straight, on their farm in Exeter, Rhode Island. His infant son, Charles, was placed in the care of his Angeline's parents, John

The birthplace of Albert Aaron Straight, Exeter, Rhode Island

and Susan Tillinghast, in West Greenwich, Rhode Island.

In the dimly lit hospital room, Albert Straight opened his eyes. He gingerly reached for his diary laying on his bed. He had been religiously keeping a daily log of his service since the day he left Rhode Island. He summoned the energy to flip through the worn and somewhat dilapidated pages, scanning his entries as they unfolded in his mind like scenes from a play. He recalled the daily drills at Camp Sprague and the first tedious march to Poolesville, Maryland. He relived how sick he was in early February 1862 when dysentery and measles sent him to the hospital for almost two weeks. He remembered the wounded soldiers coming back from Ball's Bluff and visiting them in the hospital. He imagined the warmth of the crackling fire he made in the small mud cabin he built with his friend, Caleb H.H. Greene to ward off the cold nights in camp. He could hear the bugle call and the gallop of horses as he was ordered to the front. He was haunted by the hard fighting he had experienced during the siege of Yorktown, Fair Oaks, Savage Station, the Peninsula Campaign, Mechanicsville, Fredericksburg, and Antietam. In between marches and battles, he would send dozens of letters home to his brother, John, along with his military wages to support the well-being of his children. Occasionally, he would buy his own food and could taste the soft white bread he would purchase for six cents a loaf. He remembered the pride he had in being made Sergeant in May 1862 and the joy he experienced when he received packages overflowing with food and clothing from his parents and siblings back home. All these experiences seemed to rise like smoke from a campfire filling his memory with longing, nostalgia, and melancholy. As he peered out the small window now at the growing darkness that had settled across the countryside, he could hear the faint report of an artillery piece far off in the distance. That one sound, that familiar concussion of the gun's blast, sent Straight's mind spiraling back to the events of Friday, July 3, 1863.

It was around 1:00 p.m. on July 3rd, when the Confederate Artillery preceding Pickett's charge, bombarded the Union cannoneers on Cemetery Ridge at Gettysburg.

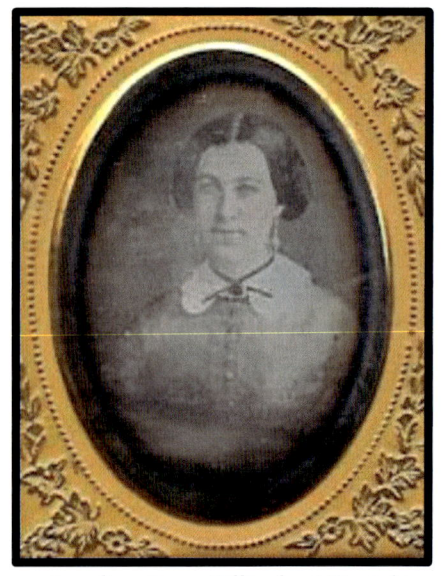

Angeline Avery Tillinghast Straight

That afternoon, Sergeant Straight was in command of Battery B's fourth gun anchored along Cemetery Ridge with the 2nd Corps. In the 85-degree heat and humidity, he quickly surveyed his gun crew, which was positioned next to a clump of trees in the center of the Union battle line. He took note first of his tent mate and close friend, Alfred Gardner, who had taken up the number two position on the gun and stood ready to place another shot in the muzzle of the cannon's tube. Standing opposite Private Gardner was William Jones who had just stepped into the number one position, relieving a fellow exhausted cannoneer. Straight then glanced over at

John Greene, with lanyard in hand, waiting anxiously as the number four man, to fire the gun once the shot was in place. Standing close by was James M. Dye of the 140th Pennsylvania Infantry, who was on detached service as Straight's gunner. He would struggle to ensure the gun's aim was accurate in the thick smoke drifting across the battlefield. Not far from Straight and his men, were the dead Battery cannoneers from the battle the day before. Straight stared at them where they mortally fell just a few yards in front of him. The corpses of Ira Bennett, Michael Flynn and David King were stiff and lifeless, decaying slowly in the hot sun.

The battle that unfolded on July 3rd was terrible beyond description. Several enemy shells were exploding in and among the Battery every minute for over an hour. There was no way to dodge the incoming missiles of death. His gun crew was taking a pounding. Several men had already been wounded and numerous horses already killed from exploding shells. In his mind though, what he remembered most was the blast that hit the cannon's muzzle. The flash and explosion were tremendous. At first, he thought his gun crew had managed to fire another shot. But as the smoke began to drift toward the trees, he knew that was not the case. He quickly realized that a Confederate shell had made a direct hit on the cannon's muzzle and then proceeded to bounce under the gun carrying away part of the axle. The aftermath of that detonation was sickening. Straight struggled to process the ghastly scene before him. The exploding shell blew twenty-five-year-old William Jones several yards forward tearing off the left side of his head, instantly killing him.

Then there was Alfred Gardner. He was sitting up against the cannon's wheel, his arm, and shoulder torn away. Sergeant Straight rushed up to his dying friend and leaning forward, struggled to hear his last words. They had promised each other that if one of them were wounded or killed, the other would come to the fallen man's side. Straight listened as Alfred Gardner gave him a message. *"Tell my wife I died happy"*, Gardner uttered. He asked that Straight send his book and bible home to his wife. Then with his remaining strength and only arm, he reached out and shook Straight's hand and said goodbye. Straight obliged his friend and told him he would send his effects home. With that, Gardner shouted *"Glory to God! Alleluia, I am happy. Amen"* and died amidst the roar of cannon fire. In disbelief of the sudden death of his friend, Straight shot up and leaped to the front of the cannon in an attempt to reload it. With the number three man wounded, James M. Dye, tore off a piece of his shirt, grabbed a rock and laid it over the cannon's open vent to prevent embers from igniting.

Straight grabbed the solid shot, ripped off the sabot, threw it to the ground, and then rammed the powder bag down the tube. Amidst flying bullets and exploding shells, he then tried to ram the solid ball down the gun's intensely hot barrel. Dye struggled to hold the ball in place as Straight swung the rammer trying to force the projectile down the gun's barrel. Lieutenant Charles A. Brown shouted for someone to grab an axe from the caisson so Straight could hit the ball and force it down the throat of the cannon. But just as Straight was striking his target with the axe, another shell made a direct hit on the battered gun, knocking out a spoke, raising the gun on one side, and mortally wounding the number four-man, John Greene. As these events transpired, the cannon now heated from heavy use began to cool and permanently clamped down on the shot now stuck in the muzzle of the gun.

At that moment, Straight heard the voice of the 2nd Corps Artillery Chief Henry Hunt as he galloped up to Battery B's position. He could see the Battery was nearly ruined and its ammunition virtually expended. In addition to the three enemy shells that struck Straight's gun, there were also more than thirty-nine bullet holes that riddled the cannon's bloodied and damaged carriage. The Battery B cannoneers were quickly ordered to the Union rear. Through the heavy smoke and burning air, Confederate Artillery officers witnessed Battery B's withdrawal from the field. At the same time, Federal Artillery fire began to slacken and fade away. The Battery's withdrawal to the rear had a dramatic effect even though they were now out of commission. Confederate generals thought that the Union line was pulling back and were convinced that the time had come to launch their grand ground assault.

Gettysburg Gun on display in front of the Old State House Providence, Rhode Island

When the attack ceased later that afternoon, Straight went back to the bloodied battlefield to retrieve implements and equipment left behind. Approaching the Battery's position earlier in the day, he paused as he saw the lifeless and now bloated body of his friend, Alfred Gardner. Sergeant Straight requested that another Battery comrade, Calvin Macomber, retrieve the small book and bible from Gardner's pocket. The next morning, in a drenching rainstorm, Straight went back again to the field with a detachment of men to bury the dead. Upon arriving at the Battery's previous position held the day before, he was aghast and grieved by the carnage left behind. The dead were scattered like autumn leaves over the trampled and burned-out grass. Their legs and arms were positioned at odd angles. Once so full of life, these bodies were now abandoned shells left to rot in the pouring rain. Straight glanced over at the body of Alfred Gardner, his once gentle and kind countenance, now bluish-purple and frozen in a rigid scowl. His eyes were wide open, staring up as if in a final lamenting plea to the heavens.

William Jones's corpse was ghastly. Blackened blood traced what was left of his nearly decapitated head. His lifeless body lay in a tangled and twisted heap in the wet grass. Straight did all he could to give them both a decent burial. He wrapped them in a red woolen blanket and buried them in the same grave near a stone wall close to where they were killed. He marked their names on a piece of wood along with the designation of Battery B First Rhode Island. Thirteen days later, on July 16, 1863, Sergeant Straight wrote to Adelia Gardner telling her that her husband had been killed, that he died happy, and enclosed the bible as requested. In the letter, he said Gardner *"flinched not when the missiles of death flew thick about us"* and told the now widowed Adelia, where he had buried her husband. On the hot morning of August 24, 1863, Straight wrote home to his brother, John. *"I often think of the dying exclamation of Alfred Gray Gardner who was shot at my piece at Gettysburg. His arm and shoulder was shot away: he lived long enough to shout Glory to God, Hallelujah, Amen and wanted I should take a bible from his pocket and send it to his wife and say to her he died happy. This same shot took the head off of another man, William Jones. I was literally covered with blood and brains, but still unharmed. I have many reasons to thank the Almighty."* Following the battle, progressively throughout August and September 1863, Straight's health deteriorated. At times, he was unable to march and was forced to ride in the Battery's wagon or ambulance. In early November, he wrote what would be his last letter to his brother, John. *"If it would be that I should not live I suppose you will be written to immediately and I want you to notify the folks and have some suitable person come after my body. But I have as much expectation of getting well now as have had for the last three weeks."* That expectation would not come to pass. Straight's condition would steadily worsen. Just as Battery B had taken a beating on Cemetery Ridge five months earlier, the cells of his intestinal wall were being ruthlessly attacked by bacterial parasites. The bacteria deliberately injected lethal toxins and poisons into his cells causing the fluids to spill out. As these unrelenting assaults continued, his frail intestines failed to properly absorb the water as they should. Instead of the food getting drier as it was digested, it would remain liquid, which would cause Sergeant Straight to ultimately suffer severe dehydration. Throughout the evening of November 15th, Straight gradually and steadily slipped away. At first, death approached slowly in the same short, shallow, and ragged breaths that claimed his wife three years earlier. The nurses on Ward A would routinely descend on Straight and listen for his breathing. They could perceive his own distinctive features now lit up by the moonlight drifting in through the window: his slightly squarish face; his deep-set eyes; his black bushy eyebrows; his bearded cheeks and; his thick hair matted from perspiration. His chest would heave then weakly relax as oxygen was slowly being ripped from his tired lungs. At 4:15 in the morning on Monday, November 16, 1863, Sergeant Albert Straight's heart would beat one last time. He died alone on Ward A at the Fairfax Seminary Hospital.

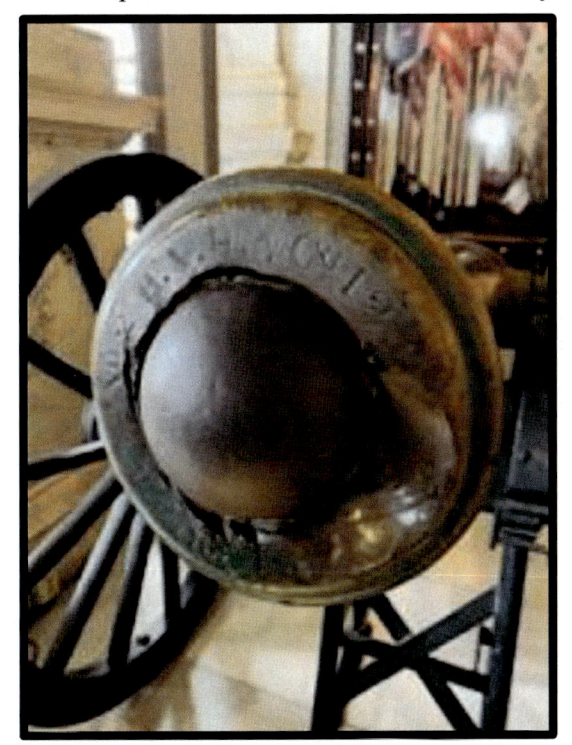

Gettysburg Gun on display at the Rhode Island State House

Laura Amanda Straight

That same day, several hospital stewards had his body prepared and shipped home to Exeter, Rhode Island through the Adams Express Company. The paperwork for his final journey home listed the wooden coffin's fragile freight as *"Sergeant Albert Straight"* and was addressed to his father-in-law, Reverend John Tillinghast. Along with his body, the nurses neatly packed his only belongings: one knapsack, one cap, two blankets, one pair of boots, one jacket, two socks, two shirts, and $29.05 in cash. When his body finally arrived by train, his family retrieved him and his meager belongings. His body was carried to the Plain Meeting House, where family and friends mourned his death and provided comfort to his orphan children who sat silently beside his wooden coffin. On September 19, 1864, fifty-one-year-old John Tillinghast and sixty-three-year-old Aaron Straight filed for a military pension for Albert Straight's orphaned son and daughter at the Rhode Island Supreme Court. Straight's former comrade and good friend, Caleb H.H. Greene would accompany the elderly men, and serve as a witness to the life and superior service of his childhood friend, Albert Straight. Reverend John Tillinghast would go on to receive the $8 a month pension for both minor children.

Both sets of grandparents respectively filed to be the legal guardians for their young grandchildren and raised them as their own until adulthood. Ten years later, in 1874, Sergeant Straight's fourth gun, with the ball still stuck in the muzzle was moved from the Navy Yard in Washington, DC, back to Rhode Island. Today, that artillery piece, now famously known as the *"Gettysburg Gun,"* sits proudly in the main foyer of the Rhode Island State House still bearing the ancient scars of July 3, 1863, when Sergeant Straight was in command.

Sergeant Albert Aaron Straight, is laid to rest next to his beloved wife, Angeline Straight at the Plain Meeting House Cemetery in West Greenwich, Rhode Island.

Our Story

The Plain Meeting House, West Greenwich, Rhode Island

Plain Meeting House Cemetery, West Greenwich, Rhode Island

Tombstones of Albert and Angeline Straight, Plain Meeting House Cemetery, West Greenwich, Rhode Island

Notes:
1. John H. Rhodes, *The History of Battery B, First Regiment Rhode Island Light Artillery* (Providence: Snow and Farnum, Printers, 1894) 202, 206-214
2. The Diary of Albert Straight from the Battery B First Rhode Island Light Artillery Incorporated Collection
3. The Letters of Albert Aaron Straight, Battery B First Rhode Island Light Artillery Incorporated Collection
4. http://muttermuseum.org/static/media/uploads/civilwar_lp9_fnl.pdf
5. William W. Kittridge Letter dated July 29, 1905 to Charles Tillinghast Straight, First Rhode Island Battery B Inc. Collection
6. https://books.google.com/books/about/Records_of_the_Bailey_Family.html?id=jdcUAAAAYAAJ
7. https://www.thecut.com/2016/06/diarrhea-is-the-wartime-enemy-no-one-mentions.html
8. https://southcarolina1670.wordpress.com/2014/11/25/gettysburg-gun-represents-rare-bit-of-rhode-island-us-history/
9. Photo of Albert Aaron Straight courtesy of Steve Allanson
10. Photo of Angeline Avery Straight courtesy of Steve Allanson
11. Waud, Alfred R. (between 1860 and 1865), Fairfax Seminary now General Hospital Headquarters for the Army of the Potomac, Retrieved from Library of Congress, https://www.loc.gov/pictures/item/2004660142/
12. Photo of Gettysburg Gun outside Rhode Island State House, courtesy of the Victor Cantoni Collection
13. All other photos courtesy of Battery B First Rhode Island Light Artillery, Inc. Collection

CHARLES DEXTER WORTHINGTON

33

An Original Member

Charles Worthington was born on January 21, 1831, in Southbridge, Massachusetts to parents Orrin Shaler Worthington and Sussana Whittemore. Charles was one of twelve children. He and seven of his brothers all served during the Civil War.

At a young age, his family moved from Southbridge to Spencer, Massachusetts, where Charles learned the trade of a weaver and worked at one of the village's mills. On August 1, 1850, Reverend Constantine Blodgett married nineteen-year-old Charles and twenty-year-old Amanda M. Eldridge at the Congregational Church in Pawtucket, Rhode Island. They lived for a short time in Spencer, Massachusetts, and then returned to Pawtucket, Rhode Island, where they would take up residence for 15 years. It was during this time that Charles and Amanda Worthington adopted a baby girl, Georgianna S. Worthington, born on November 15, 1855.

When the Civil War erupted in April 1861, Charles was employed as a jeweler but quickly felt impelled to serve the Union cause. On August 13, 1861, Charles exchanged goodbyes with his wife and young daughter and volunteered as a private with Battery B First Rhode Island Light Artillery in Providence, Rhode Island. A couple months later he was promoted to corporal on October 1, 1861. He would go on to serve in every major battle with Battery B. He saw action in battles including Ball's Bluff, the Siege of Yorktown, Fair Oaks, Savage's Station, Malvern Hill, Chapman's Farm, White Oak Swamp, Gettysburg, the Wilderness, Spotsylvania, Cold Harbor, and the five battles around Petersburg. He was wounded at Gettysburg on July 2, 1863, and again at the battle of The Wilderness on May 5, 1864. Worthington bravely served his entire three-year enlistment and was mustered out of federal service on August 12, 1864.

When Charles returned home from the war, he found employment as a stationary engineer in Steubenville, Ohio. In 1870, he and his wife and his daughter moved back to Spencer, Massachusetts, where he worked as an engineer for the Spencer Fire Department. Tragically, their only daughter, Georgianna, would die at the age of eighteen on February 22, 1873. A year later in 1874, Worthington would be reunited with his Battery B comrades as a member of the Battery B Veteran Association. From 1874 until his death in 1916, he attended each of their annual reunions. He faithfully served on multiple committees to preserve the history of Battery B. Oddly enough however, though he served in every major engagement and mustered in as an original member of Battery B, Charles Worthington's name was incorrectly omitted from the list of original members in Battery B's Regimental History published in 1894. He died on November 15, 1916. He was 85 years old.

Charles and his wife, Amanda, are buried at Pine Grove Cemetery in Spencer, Massachusetts.

Burial site of Corporal Charles Worthington, Pine Grove Cemetery, Spencer, Massachusetts

Notes:
1. John H. Rhodes, *The History of Battery B, First Regiment Rhode Island Light Artillery* (Providence: Snow and Farnum, Printers, 1894) 356
2. https://www.genealogy.com/ftm/w/o/r/Patricia-Worthington-Michigan/GENE1-0001.html
3. The "Springfield Republican" Newspaper, dated August 2, 1900, article entitled, "Golden Wedding at Spencer".
4. Photo of Worthington courtesy of Battery B First Rhode Island Light Artillery Inc. Collection

HENRY HOSEA BALLOU

34

A Fallen Son

On Tuesday, September 23, 1862, seven days after the bloodiest day of the Civil War, Private Henry Hosea Ballou wrote home to his father in Rhode Island. *"It was a horrid sight to look over the battlefield and see some three or four hundred dead men on both sides lying in a cornfield."*

A little over a year before that horrific day, the young and well-educated Ballou was living with his parents and his three sisters in Rhode Island. Henry had celebrated his 18th birthday one day before the Civil War began on April 12, 1861, when Fort Sumter came under attack. A printer by trade, Ballou no doubt knew the significance of that attack and the war that would follow. As April gave way to August 1861, Ballou, like many other young men, felt the strong pull to enlist in the Union Army. On August 13, 1861, with the guarantee of a $15 enlistment bonus, Henry volunteered as a private with Battery B First Rhode Island Light Artillery at the Benefit Street Arsenal in Providence. He promised his father he would write home often.

Today, 26 letters written in near-perfect penmanship survive through the care of Ballou's descendants. These letters vividly illustrate how this heroic young man experienced the burdens and sufferings of the war. His letters tell of the privations of a soldier's life and often request the necessities and comforts from home. His wishes include a pair of boots, stationery, stamps, a tobacco pipe, a songbook, even a remedy of rum and sulfur for his acne that was aggravated during the hot summer months. He asked for fresh food and complained of *"bread so hard that all the devils in hell could not tread it fine in a month."*

Henry would get his first taste of battle at Ball's Bluff on October 21, 1861. The battle was a Union disaster and Battery B's losses during that engagement were significant. Ballou's account of the scene is captivating. *"It was as cold as Greenland, being so near the water and the wind blowed down the river in a perfect hurricane…It began to rain in perfect torrents…The island was a perfect sea of mud."* So muddy in fact, Ballou complained that even the coffee had a muddy after taste. *"The bullets were coming like a shower of rain among us"*, he continued. *"They were whistling thick and fast around us [and] cut the limbs of trees over our heads."* Despite the terrifying conditions and suffering that accompanied everyday life as a soldier, Henry was determined to see the war through. In January 1862, he expressed his thoughts to his father writing, *"when I leave the army it will be when the war is over and not before."* In December 1862, at the battle of Fredericksburg, Ballou would experience some of the fiercest fighting of the war. In the midst of the battle, Ballou would be hit in the hip by a spent mini-ball that had passed through the side of another soldier. Somehow, Ballou survived that day and would go on serving the Union cause.

Throughout the winter and spring of 1862, Ballou's letters to his father expressed a wide array of sentiments. In some ways he was prophetic, knowing that the odds were against him surviving the entire war. At other times, he communicated his love for the Union and his duty and honor to preserve it. And most importantly, he wrote of having hope. Ballou hoped that he would be granted a furlough and be able to go home and visit his father, who by this time, had become a widower. At one point he wrote his father that to be a soldier it takes, *"a man with an iron frame and the patience of Job."* Ballou no doubt exhibited those qualities having been made a corporal on January 31, 1863, and promoted again to lance sergeant on May 16, 1863.

His last letter home was dated March 17, 1863. In it, he thanked his father for a new pair of boots and expressed optimism in returning to his native Rhode Island in the coming months. But four months later, on July 2, 1863, Ballou would be mortally wounded during the Battle of Gettysburg. Serving as the gunner on the first gun under Sergeant John Wardlow, Ballou was shot as the Battery was forced to remove their guns from the field after coming into close fighting with a brigade from Georgia who swarmed the Battery's position. Corporal Ballou was rushed to a nearby field hospital and clung to life for two days until July 4, 1863, when he finally succumbed to his wounds. He was twenty-years-old at the time of his death.

Upon learning that his son had been killed, his father, Joseph Ballou, tried to retrieve his body and finally bring him home. A friend of the Ballou family was sent to perform the grim task but, ultimately, Henry's body could not be located in the post-battle chaos. Eventually, laborers under the direction of Samuel Weaver, would exhume Ballou's body and inter him in the Soldiers National Cemetery at Gettysburg where he lies in repose today. Corporal Ballou's inconsolable and heartbroken father would die just two years later in 1865 a month before the Confederate Army's flag of truce dipped below Battery B's guidon on its way towards Appomattox Court House, Virginia, and the end of the Civil War.

Henry Hosea Ballou gravesite at the Soldiers National Cemetery, Gettysburg

Notes:
1. John H. Rhodes, *The History of Battery B, First Regiment Rhode Island Light Artillery* (Providence: Snow and Farnum, Printers, 1894) 357
2. Whitaker, Lee Robert. "Letters from Sergeant Ballou Civil War and remembrance". *Providence Journal*, May 25, 1997, Vol. CXI No. 21
3. Photo of Grave credited to Sophia Isabel Evangelista
4. Photo of Henry Hosea Ballou, Henry Hosea Ballou family archives, courtesy of Lee Whitaker, a descendant of Joseph R. and Ruth M. Ballou

STILLMAN HARRISON BUDLONG

35

The Diary

Stillman Harrison Budlong died more than 147 years ago, but his voice can still be heard today. Despite the long passage of time since his service with Battery B First Rhode Island Light Artillery, Stillman's words echo throughout the decades, thanks to the preservation of his diaries that he faithfully kept during the Civil War.

Budlong was a native of Warwick, Rhode Island. He was born on September 2, 1841, to parents William and Abby (Peabody) Budlong. Like other young men at the time, Budlong attended school and aspired to become a machinist. But as national tensions increased and war between the states broke out, Budlong put his personal aspirations on hold. Instead, just a few weeks shy of his 20th birthday, he enlisted with Battery B as an original member on August 13, 1861. That same day, Budlong began his diary with the following entry, *"was sworn into the service of the United States of America about 3 p.m."*

It is not clear why the young soldier began keeping his journal. Perhaps it was an attempt to capture his thoughts, or maybe it was an effort to record the unprecedented war that was unfolding around him. Regardless of the reason, his diaries remain an invaluable historical record of what life must have been like with Battery B. His entries, written nearly every day over a three-year period from 1861-1864, are at once mundane and profound expressing both private and universal thoughts. His writing style is short and succinct but provides remarkable clarity about his experience as a soldier. Each note offers a snapshot, a historical window into his life while in service to the Union Army.

Many of his day-to-day recollections are only a line or two, *"went after hay, killed a hog our boys did, and had a fuss about it, went after sweet potatoes, did not get any but got wet though."* Sometimes the only thing of mention in his journal is the weather, *"pleasant and warm"* or *"cloudy and chilly."* One entry reads, *"Hardest rain and hailstorm I ever saw, the stones were an inch in diameter."* At other times, he often writes about his daily duties: Drilling, standing guard duty, taking care of the horses, marching, setting up camp, foraging for supplies, and of course, writing home to his many family members and friends, Mother, Mary, Anna, and George.

His diary includes unique anecdotes. One such story describes a harrowing journey down the Potomac River aboard the *Julia Maine* that the helmsman could not steer, crashing the ship into a drawbridge. In another entry, he writes that his fellow soldiers were poisoned. The boys, *"were sick by drinking drugged beer."* When they caught and arrested the man who sold the beer, it was Budlong who stood guard over him. Budlong also includes mention of his duties assisting the Battery

B cook. One entry reads, *"Helped the cook make doughnuts - had 16 each man."* With the $12 monthly wage, Budlong also looked for ways to earn more money. *"Sold 2 lbs. of cakes made $7.55 sent money home."* He also traded food when he could. *"Traded rice for pies (living high for soldiers)."*

Stillman's diary at times is more of a map than a journal. He describes every instance the Battery was on the move through Virginia, Maryland and Pennsylvania. One entry tells of his excursions to the White House and the Smithsonian while stationed in the nation's capital. With supplies and equipment often hard to come by, and the weather often cold, little things made a big difference. Budlong recorded in the fall of 1861, *"I got a red blanket, yes I did, from U.S."* At other times, his entries provide a personal portrait of the young man. In July 1862, he recorded this important milestone, *"Shaved for the first time since I came out."*

These everyday occurrences help paint the picture of a soldier, who was wildly observant, extremely industrious, exceptionally honest, and most of all, genuinely hopeful that one day he would be granted a furlough and return home to his family. He writes, *"Lieut Brown promised he would try and get me a furlough as soon as he could."* But furloughs were hard to come by in 1863. Budlong recounts that only 2 out of every 100 men were allowed that privilege. Beyond these long odds, a furlough always seemed slightly out of reach, largely in part to his own clumsy lack of discipline. Several times Stillman is forced to 'carry a rail' for several hours as a punishment for not following orders or for being away from camp. *"I left the battery to get some apples and what else I could find; got on the wrong road…could not find the battery."* The next day around mid-morning he found Battery B, but was punished for being lost. *"Had to take care of the spare horses; finished by carrying a rail till 12 at night."*

Budlong's diary also reveals first-hand accounts and important events. During the fall of 1862, Budlong narrates that, *"Ole Abe, Gen McClellan and Gen Sumner rode through our camp."*

There are also several notes about his first-hand experience in battle. A day after the battle of Fair Oaks and Seven Pines, his description reads, *"went over the battleground, awful night. There were dead everywhere and in all kind of shape. Buried about all the dead."* Later at the Battle of Malvern Hill, Budlong recounts a brush with death, *"One shell exploded within 10 feet of me."* When Budlong and Battery B arrived at the battle at Antietam, his entry describes the brutal scene, *"went on the trot with the shell bursting and whizzing around us."*

At Gettysburg, Budlong's July 3, 1863, entry provides an eye-witness account of the carnage. *"In the afternoon the rebs opened up on us with 104 guns (so prisoner's say) and we returned the fire and kept it up till our ammunition was most all gone when we was ordered to limber to the rear…it was the heaviest firing I ever saw and the generals say the same. They had 4 crossfires on us. It was awful. We was ordered back about 3 miles and stopped there all night."* Budlong survived Gettysburg and would go on to fight throughout the rest of the war. He was made a corporal on May 12, 1864. Six days later, he would be wounded in a skirmish, but again, survive. He was mustered out of federal service on August 12, 1865. A year later, he married Anna Buell, with whom he had corresponded throughout the war. Together they would have three children. As a civilian, Budlong eventually became a machinist and later became the first janitor of the Elm Street School in Westerly, Rhode Island around 1870. His employment there, however, would not last long. Three years later on October 1, 1873, Stillman died at the young age of 32. His wife, Anna, would pass away nine years later on February 2, 1882. Stillman and Anna Budlong are buried at River Bend Cemetery in Westerly, Rhode Island.

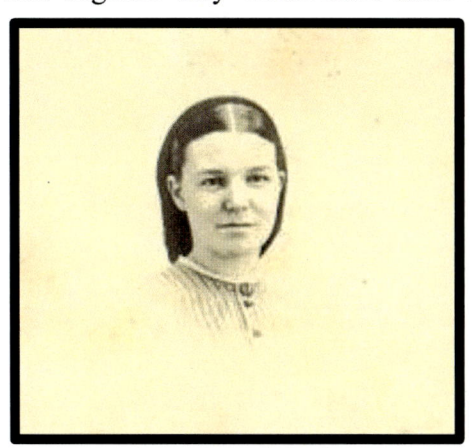

Anna M. Buell Budlong

Headstone of Stillman Harrison Budlong, River Bend Cemetery, Westerly, Rhode Island

Notes:
1. John H. Rhodes, *The History of Battery B, First Regiment Rhode Island Light Artillery* (Providence: Snow and Farnum, Printers, 1894) 67, 289, 357
2. Stillman Harrison Budlong Civil War Diaries, courtesy of Westerly Library, Westerly Rhode Island
3. *Find a Grave*, database and images (https://www.findagrave.com: accessed 21 November 2022), memorial page for Anna M Buell Budlong (13 Nov 1845-2 Feb 1882), Find a Grave Memorial no. 129033995, citing River Bend Cemetery, Westerly, Washington County, Rhode Island, USA, photograph by William P. Jones.
4. Find a Grave, database and images (https://findagrave.com: accessed 21 November 2020, memorial page for Stillman Harrison Budlong (1841 -1 Oct 1873), Find a Grave Memorial No. 129033997, citing River Bend Cemetery, Westerly, Washington County, Rhode Island, USA; Photo by Jane Ferner Lawrence
5. Photo of Anna Buell Budlong with permission from William P. Jones

JOHN HENRY RHODES

Our Story

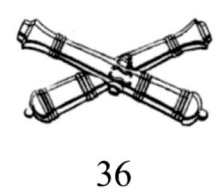

36

The Regimental History

John Henry Rhodes was mustered into federal service with Battery B First Rhode Island Light Artillery on August 13, 1861. At the time of his enlistment, the twenty-year-old private with light brown hair and blue eyes, would have never dreamed that someday he would be responsible for authoring Battery B's regimental history, nearly thirty years later.

Rhodes was the son of Benjamin and Sarah Rhodes and at the time of his enlistment with the Union artillery, he was married to his young wife, Cynthia A. Baxter. A day after his enlistment on August 14, 1861, Rhodes and roughly 135 soldiers waved goodbye to their family and friends at Exchange Place in Providence, Rhode Island, and boarded a train toward Washington, DC. Cynthia would not be in the crowd that day. Instead, she gave birth to their daughter, Marcia Cynthia Rhodes.

Rhodes served in every major engagement with Battery B from Ball's Bluff in 1861 to Petersburg in 1864. Early on in his service, he was promoted to lance corporal on November 18, 1862, and a year later, he was made corporal on October 7, 1863. Three days after his promotion, Rhodes and his comrades were forced to witness a terrible scene. *"On the forenoon of the 10th, the brigade was called out and assembled on the plain near headquarters to witness a somewhat sad and novel scene, namely: the branding and drumming out of service of deserters from one of the batteries. The brigade was formed into a hollow square facing inward, with a battery forge in the centre, the blacksmith blowing the bellows. The deserters were brought into the square under an infantry guard and took position near the forge. The deserters were then partially stripped of their clothing, irons were heated and the letter "D" was burned upon their left hip. Their heads were shaven after which they were marched about the square under guard, led by a corp of fife and drummers playing the "Rogue's March". It was a painful and humiliating sight, but undoubtedly left its salutary impression, as was designed, upon all who witnessed it."*

Rhodes was eventually promoted to sergeant on November 24, 1863, replacing Sergeant Straight who died on November 16, 1863, and served with the Battery until he was mustered out of service on August 12, 1864. After the war, Rhodes returned home to Olneyville, Rhode Island, and resumed his civilian life with his wife and daughter. His home life however, would be tragically altered a little more than a year later. On Wednesday, October 25, 1865, Cynthia Rhodes died from complications of pneumonia and typhoid. His young bride was just 20-years-old at the time of her death leaving the young veteran a widower. John Rhodes eventually re-married

Emma Nye in November 1865 and together they had one son, Waldo Prescott Rhodes on February 25, 1871. In 1880, Rhodes took an active part in the membership of the Battery B Veteran Association serving as both secretary and treasurer. Perhaps his most significant contribution to the Battery, however, was his authorship of the Battery B Regimental History. During the 1880s the veterans of Battery B expressed an interest to record their experiences during the Civil War. In 1875, veterans Gideon Spencer, Rowland Dodge and, Daniel Taylor were appointed by the members of the Battery B Veteran Association to the Historical Committee to collect Battery B history, records, and accounts of their service. Five years later, the Committee reported that no progress had been made. Despite the lack of advancement, John Delevan stepped up and tried to carry on the work of writing the regimental history. But by 1890, Delevan too fell short and reported that there was no hope of producing such a record for the battery.

A year later, on March 28, 1891, during a meeting of the Executive Committee for the Battery B Veteran Association, Rhodes proposed to publish a history of the Battery taking on any costs associated with the task. The Association voted to accept the offer, and Rhodes made an earnest plea to have all the veterans turn over to him any records and materials they might have to help write this historical narrative. Despite deafness in his left ear and ongoing vision issues, Rhodes successfully published the Battery's Regimental History in 1894. In his short preface, he describes his thoughts and objectives. *"As author, I make no claim to possess special qualifications for the work assumed, but being situated so that I could give the time which the work required, I have endeavored to bring to the front the honorable part borne by Battery B."* He goes on to write, *"The work is a plain statement of facts connected with the service of the organization, and if it proves satisfactory in a reasonable degree to the survivors and the public, I shall feel fully compensated for the labor."* In the years after John H. Rhodes published the Battery's regimental history, his health significantly declined. In 1898, he passed out while watering his grass, breaking his right ankle in the process. In 1901, Rhodes was diagnosed with congestive heart disease. In addition to these ailments, Rhodes was also being treated for carcinoma on his right cheek. The veteran endured three painful operations but, ultimately, these procedures were unsuccessful. On Wednesday, June 12, 1901, John Rhodes passed away quietly at his home on Penn Street in Providence. He was just 59 years old. He is buried along with his wife at the North Burial Ground, Providence, Rhode Island.

John H. Rhodes, Author of the Battery B Regimental History

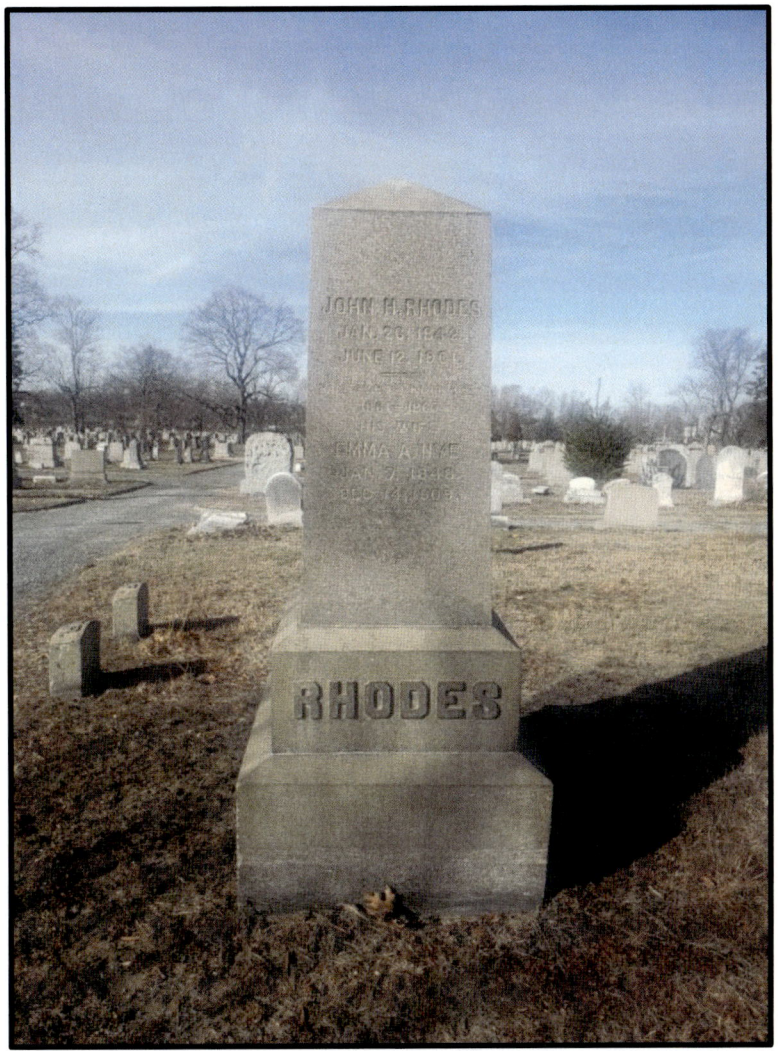

Grave belonging to John Rhodes, North Burial Ground, Providence, Rhode Island

Notes:
1. John H. Rhodes, *The History of Battery B, First Regiment Rhode Island Light Artillery* (Providence: Snow and Farnum, Printers, 1894) i-ix, iii-iv, 241, 355
2. All photos courtesy of Battery B First Rhode Island Light Artillery Inc. Collection

LEVI JOHNSON CORNELL

37

The Gettysburg Gun

The *Gettysburg* Gun, a bronze Napoleon cannon, proudly sits today inside the main public entrance of the Rhode Island State House. This 1200-pound gun, mounted on its original wooden carriage, still bears its ancient wounds suffered more than 150 years ago. It was last fired on July 3, 1863, at Gettysburg, where it was struck three times by Confederate shells and hit with 39 bullets. During the battle, one of those Confederate shells struck the muzzle of the cannon. The direct hit dented the muzzle and killed two of Battery B's artillerists. Following the blast, members of Battery B, including Sergeant Albert Straight, tried to drive a solid shot down the barrel with an axe but, the ball would not move past the dented muzzle. As the gun cooled, the solid ball became welded in place. With the piece disabled, Battery B would be ordered to limber to the rear with the solid shot still lodged in the mouth of Sergeant Straight's fourth gun. This cannon, however, and its story, would have been lost to history if it were not for Levi J. Cornell.

Cornell was born in Connecticut in May 1844. At the age of 17, he signed up to volunteer as an original member with Battery B on August 13, 1861. He served as a driver, mounted atop one of the Battery's horse teams that were used to pull the cannons during the war's many campaigns. He saw battle in nearly every major engagement with Battery B, including the major battles at Ball's Bluff, Seven Pines, Savage Station, Malvern Hill, South Mountain, Antietam, Fredericksburg, Gettysburg, Mine Run, and the Wilderness. But it was his actions after the battle at Gettysburg that helped preserve the first relic of the war, the *Gettysburg Gun*.

On the afternoon of July 3, 1863, the Gettysburg countryside was a scene of death and destruction. Battery B's losses during the battle were a microcosm of the epic engagement. Battery B had lost seven men killed, thirty-one men wounded, and one man was taken prisoner. In addition, there were twenty-nine horses killed and another thirty-six wounded. This would have been the grisly scene that Cornell witnessed on that hot July afternoon. He and another fellow driver, Charles Fried, had been ordered to remove the disabled fourth gun from the field.

Amid the flying shrapnel, exploding shells and, whizzing mini balls, Cornell drove his remaining horse team off the field dragging the battered cannon behind him. In the confusion and chaos of the moment, he drove his horse team north into the town of Gettysburg instead of heading south to the artillery reserve, where the remaining and beleaguered Battery B artillerists were regrouping after the battle. He rode for several hours trying to locate Battery B but was unsuccessful. As the afternoon wore on into the evening, Cornell and Fried were forced to give up their search and decided to camp for the night in the woods. The next morning as a steady rain began to drench the roads and fields, they resumed their search and finally delivered the gun safely into the hands of Battery B by mid-morning.

When they arrived in the artillery camp, the men were astonished to see the condition of the gun and joked with Cornell for getting lost, asking if he had been to Baltimore since the fight. As the soldiers gathered around the gun and examined its bullet holes and the fused solid shot in the muzzle, Cornell explained what happened and how they took a wrong turn amidst the fighting the day before. The cannon was eventually condemned and sent to Washington D.C., where it was placed on exhibition until May 1874 and then subsequently returned to Rhode Island through the efforts of the Battery B Veteran Association. In 1962, nearly 100 years after the battle, officials realized that there was still a two-pound bag of highly explosive gun powder resting inside the cannon's tube. The Rhode Island National Guard quickly removed the gun from its perch and submerged it in a pool of water where the gun powder seeped out through a small drill hole. But the story of the *Gettysburg Gun* did not end there. In 1988, Captain Ron Tracey, Captain Phil DiMaria, and dedicated members from the newly reactivated Battery B historical organization, worked together to transport the famous gun back to its actual position on the battlefield, during the 125th Anniversary of the battle at Gettysburg. During that event, thousands of visitors were able to see the gun and the ordeal it survived more than a century earlier. The *Gettysburg Gun* journey and its place in history would not have been possible without Levi Cornell and his determination to get that gun back to the safety of Battery B and the Union artillery reserve. After the battle at Gettysburg in 1863, Cornell would serve as a driver for Battery B until May 5, 1864, when he was wounded at the Battle of the Wilderness. Though injured, he survived and lived to be mustered out of federal service a few months later on August 12, 1864. He returned to Richmond, Rhode Island, and farmed his land. He would later go on to serve as the first Postmaster of the Kenyon, Rhode Island Post Office. Cornell died at the age of 63 on March 29, 1908. He is buried at Wickes Cemetery, Coventry, Rhode Island.

The Veterans of Battery B at the Benefit Street Arsenal during an 1882 reunion with the Gettysburg Gun.

Members of Battery B First Rhode Island Re-Enactment Group at the 125 Gettysburg Anniversary with the Gettysburg Gun, 1988

Notes:
1. John H. Rhodes, *The History of Battery B, First Regiment Rhode Island Light Artillery* (Providence: Snow and Farnum, Printers, 1894) 216, 275, 317
2. https://southcarolina1670.wordpress.com/2014/11/25/gettysburg-gun-represents-rare-bit-of-rhode-island-us-history/
3. https://www.providencejournal.com/news/20170702/on-gettysburg-anniversary-cannon-in-ri-has-story-to-tell
4. http://thesaltysailor.com/rhodeisland-philatelic/rhodeisland/settle-30.htm
5. *Find a Grave,* database and images (https://www.findagrave.com: accessed 29 November 2020), memorial page for Levi Johnson Cornell (31 May 1844–20 Mar 1908), Find a Grave Memorial no. 90820946, citing Wickes Cemetery, Coventry, Kent County, Rhode Island, USA; Maintained by Michael Paton (contributor 47042047).
6. Photo of Battery B Re-Enactment Group with the *Gettysburg Gun* courtesy of the Battery B First Rhode Island Light Artillery Inc. Collection
7. Photo of 1882 Battery B Reunion courtesy of the Battery B First Rhode Island Light Artillery Inc. Collection

ALBERT JENCKES WHIPPLE

38

"Stunned and Dazed"

In February 1908, from his room at the National Soldiers Home in Togus, Maine, 70-year-old Albert Whipple penned a short note describing his experience at the battle of Gettysburg, to his friend, Charles Tillinghast Straight. For two long hot days in July 1863, Battery B First Rhode Island Light Artillery found itself locked in a deadly confrontation that shook the quiet Pennsylvania countryside. In his letter, he wrote, *"I remember seeing horses drop and seeing limbers and caissons explode."* At the time of the battle, Albert Whipple was just 25-years-old.

Born in Rhode Island on October 16, 1838, the son of Stephen Very Whipple and Adeline Jenckes Whipple, Albert was one of eleven children. At the outbreak of the Civil War, he left behind his carpentry trade and volunteered with Battery B First Rhode Island Light Artillery as one of the original members on August 13, 1861. Whipple served with Battery B through every major engagement from 1861-1863. Shortly after the Battle at Antietam in 1862, Whipple was appointed the lead driver of the horse team belonging to Battery B's first gun. He held that position for several months until the spring of 1863 when he fell ill with malaria. Sick with fever but not wanting to leave, Whipple struggled to keep up with the Battery on its march to Gettysburg by riding on horseback or hitching a ride on the limber chest. He made visits to the Battery doctor whenever he could, where he received doses of whiskey and quinine to aid in his recovery.

On July 2, 1863, during the Battle at Gettysburg, Whipple and the Battery's six-gun detachments tirelessly worked their cannons near a stone wall beyond the Codori Farm for as long as they could before being ordered to "limber to the rear". In the process of pulling back the guns, Whipple witnessed several of his comrades receive mortal wounds. First, there was Private David King who fell after receiving a bullet wound from the advancing ground assault carried out by Wright's Georgian Brigade. He lived a few moments before dying alone in the blazing sun. And then there was Henry Hosea Ballou, who was struck by an enemy bullet as he and others tried desperately to pull two of the remaining cannons off the field through a narrow gap in a nearby stonewall. Ballou would be carried from the field and taken to a nearby field hospital. Whipple would never see him again. Ballou died two days later. After reaching the relative safety behind the stone wall, another cannoneer, Lewis A. Moulton, Company G 19th Maine (on detached service to Battery B) was also hit and forced to dismount from his horse. Throughout that terrible afternoon, Whipple remained with his horse team and prepared for the battle that would follow the next day. The following afternoon, Albert Whipple was engaged in the great artillery struggle that unfolded on July 3, 1863.

Up and down the Union line, Federal batteries took aim at Confederate artillery positioned about a mile away on Seminary Ridge. Shortly before Battery B pulled its remaining guns from their position on the field, Whipple was hit. In his letter, he depicts that moment. *"A few moments before we left the field, a piece of shell about as big as a man's fist struck me in the left shoulder knocking me down, and knocking the wind out of me; I was so stunned and dazed I could not ride my horse, but with the help of some of the men I was able to walk down the Taneytown Road and to the place where we went into camp. I had to carry my arm in a sling several days afterward."*

Whipple would go on to survive Gettysburg and the rest of the war. He mustered out of the Battery on August 12, 1864. After his return home to Rhode Island, he married 19-year-old Medora Crosby Whipple in 1865. Sadly, two years later she died. In 1867, Whipple remarried Emily Fisk Whipple. They were married for 30 years before she too, passed away in 1897. Albert would be a widower for another 28 years before he died on April 13, 1925, at the National Soldiers Home in Maine. At the time of his death, he left behind one brother and five sisters. He is laid to rest in Cook Cemetery, Woonsocket, Rhode Island.

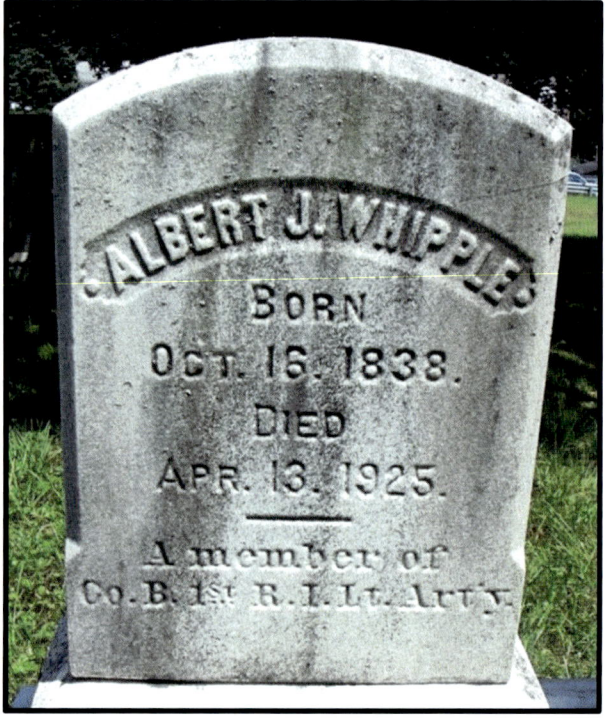

Albert Whipple Grave at Cook Cemetery, Woonsocket, Rhode Island

Notes:
1. John H. Rhodes, *The History of Battery B, First Regiment Rhode Island Light Artillery* (Providence: Snow and Farnum, Printers, 1894) 375
2. Whipple, Albert. Letter to Charles Tillinghast Straight, 3 February 1908. Courtesy of Battery B First Rhode Island Light Artillery Inc. Collection
3. *Find a Grave*, database and images (https://www.findagrave.com: accessed 05 December 2020), memorial page for Albert Jenckes Whipple (1838–13 Apr 1925), Find a Grave Memorial no. 25553736, citing Cook Cemetery, Woonsocket, Providence County, Rhode Island, USA; Photo by "Photo by brianz190".
4. Photo of Whipple courtesy of Battery B First Rhode Island Light Artillery Inc. Collection

**JOHN MAHONEY
(ALIAS WILLIAM JONES)**

39

William Jones Forever

Beneath the thick green grass in the small Rhode Island plot of the Soldiers National Cemetery in Gettysburg, is the grave of Corporal William Jones. His remains were laid to rest there more than a century and a half ago. Today, visitors and tourists, who happen to come across his grave can only observe what they see, the weathered stone and the etched engraving of his name and rank. Yet buried below the soft sod is the story of a young man whose real name was forgotten, whose identity had nearly been lost, and whose journey brought him hundreds of miles from his home to meet his death on the rolling fields of Gettysburg.

William Jones was born with the birth name, John Mahoney, on December 7, 1837, in Boston, Massachusetts. A few years before his birth, his parents immigrated to the United States from Ireland. In 1842 at the age of five, John's father suddenly died leaving his mother, Margaret, a widow. For about a year, the young woman did what she could to financially support herself and her son but, she was not able to provide for their well-being alone. Soon after, she remarried Charles Nott, a tailor, widower, and father of four children. Together they raised John and his four step-siblings in the years before the Civil War.

In early May 1861, twenty-four-year-old John Mahoney enlisted from Boston in the United States Navy. Four months after his naval enlistment, John Mahoney would enlist again with Battery B First Rhode Island Light Artillery on the morning of August 13, 1861. That morning he volunteered under the alias of William Jones. His reasoning and decisions to adopt an alias and enlist from Providence rather than Boston, remain unclear.

In August 1861 as Battery B was in the final stages of its organization, Jones shared a room in a Providence boarding house with fellow Battery B volunteer, John Delevan. On the night of the Battery's departure from Providence to Washington, DC, Jones and Delevan shared the same seat on the overcrowded train. For a long time, the two sat in silence as the train lumbered forward in the darkness. Then, Jones broke the stillness and turned to Delevan. *"Johnny, this is our going, but what will the returning be?"* Like most volunteers on that train, Jones could have never imagined what lie ahead.

Five months after enlisting in Battery B, Jones was promoted to lance corporal on December 15, 1861. He was highly regarded as one of the best artillerists in the unit being an expert in every position on the field piece. He was handy with a saber and shared his adroitness for a sword, teaching others how to use one. Throughout most of 1862, Jones experienced hard combat with Battery B during the Peninsula Campaign, the Battle of Fair Oaks and Malvern Hill. For unknown reasons, Jones was reduced to a private a few days before the battle at Antietam in September 1862. Still, Jones would perform as an excellent cannoneer with the Battery as they moved into the winter of 1862.

At Fredericksburg in December 1862, Jones and Battery B would open fire on the small Virginia town and then find themselves waiting in its streets before moving into battle. Many soldiers took this opportunity to find food or supplies in the burned-out houses before moving on. It was there that Jones found a book hidden between two beds along with some silverware. He stuffed the book into his sack coat as a memento and rejoined the Battery as they moved to the front. That day, the Battery would suffer awful casualties, but Jones would be unharmed. He would go on to fight in the Chancellorsville Campaign in May 1863. Three months later, he would find himself at the crossroads town of Gettysburg, where the Army of the Potomac and the Army of Northern Virginia would engage in an epic battle.

As darkness fell across the Gettysburg battlefield on the evening of July 2, 1863, William Jones closed his eyes. He had been up since 2 a.m. that morning when the Battery received marching orders to move up to the front and form a battle line on Cemetery Ridge. More than seventeen hours later, Jones took a deep breath and reflected on the heavy casualties that Battery B First Rhode Island Light Artillery had suffered throughout that long, hot day. He had witnessed and experienced so much. He watched as his fellow artillerist, David King, was shot dead. He heard the agonizing cries of Corporal Henry Hosea Ballou who was severely wounded and evacuated from the field. He witnessed Ira Bennett be shot and killed along with Michael Flynn. Even his commanding officer, Lieutenant Fred Brown, was blown off his horse, shot in the neck. It was a living nightmare. Sixteen others from the Battery were wounded and another captured. It was like nothing he had ever seen before and he had seen an awful lot over the last two years of service in Battery B. This battle was different. It was beyond any explanation. When he opened his eyes, he could make out the dim outline of his surviving comrades lying on their backs looking up at the evening sky. They all knew this battle was not over yet. There was more to come in the morning, perhaps much more. Jones predicted that night that he would be killed the next day. John Delevan and others tried to change his thoughts and his mind about his prescient statement, but his mind and fate were set.

The next morning Jones awoke in the early pre-dawn darkness. As he looked around at those trying to steal a few more moments of rest, he reflected on the unique moment he found himself in. There was suffering and death all around him though one thing troubled him the most. It was not the heat and humidity, though it was bad. It was not the thirst he experienced without a sip of water in the last 24 hours. The worst thing was waiting. The waiting for the groans and pleas of the wounded and dying to cease; the waiting for the Union commanders to order them into battery formation; waiting for the moment to load and fire their field pieces against those who were likewise waiting for them. Waiting was torture, and that waiting weighed on Jones throughout the morning and early afternoon hours of July 3, 1863.

To keep his mind occupied, Jones and his comrades played cards and debated about the utility of fuses behind the protection of the 12-pound Napoleon guns. But their conversation and the card game were cut short around 1:00 in the afternoon when they heard the distinctive blast of a Confederate signal gun. That one blast would unleash hell upon the Union lines for the next two hours. With the waiting over, Jones took up his position on the limber chest of the fourth gun and was soon joined by his close friend, John Delevan. Together they would rapidly cut fuses for the ammunition rounds and hand them to the number five-man, John Mowry, who was the youngest member of Battery B. It wasn't too long before Jones and Delevan ran out of ammunition. They signaled their plight to Calvin Macomber and Charles Paine, who were several yards behind them at the Battery's caisson. Macomber and Paine immediately began to prepare additional rounds and place them in the haversack of the young Mowry, who would now run a longer distance to get the ammunition to the number two man, Alfred Gardner.

John Mowry

With no ammunition left in the limber, Jones and Delevan decided to move further to the front to take up positions where men had fallen wounded or dead. Before leaving the limber though, Jones pulled from his pocket the book he found at Fredericksburg and gently placed it in the empty chest. Then he and Delevan advanced to the fourth gun commanded by Sergeant Albert Straight. To his left, Delevan could see that the third gun lacked a man at the gunner position. He nodded to Jones and then dashed to the adjacent cannon to assist Sergeant Horton, who was standing at the gun's trail. At the same moment, amidst the roaring of the artillery pieces to his left and right, Jones heard the number one man, Bob Wilkenson, calling for assistance. Jones dashed up to the exhausted Wilkenson and took the sponge staff from him. Wilkenson would walk a short distance behind the gun and then slump into the grass. Jones would swab the gun and look to his immediate left. There he would see the number two man, Alfred Gardner, preparing to load the piece. A mile away, another Confederate artillerist would pull the lanyard of his field piece. The gun would ignite and a shell would burst forth from its mouth traveling roughly 1,400 feet per second over the approximate one-mile expanse toward Battery

Charles Paine

B's position. That shell would directly strike the muzzle of Jones' gun and explode, mortally wounding Alfred Gardner. The blast and flying shrapnel would also rip a large hole into the left side of Jones's head and propel his body into the smoke-filled air. In that instant, he would experience a strange sensation. The noises around him would fall silent. The harsh burning smell would dissipate. His vision would fade to black; and his life would end while he was still airborne, dying even before his body returned to the ground.

He would remain on the battlefield for more than 14 hours before Battery B's burial crews arrived under Sergeant Albert Straight the next day, Saturday, July 4, 1863. That morning, Sergeant Straight ordered his men to bury William Jones and Alfred Gardner in the same shallow grave near a stone wall where they fell. He had them wrapped each in a red woolen blanket and placed a wooden marker in the dirt bearing their names and unit, Battery B First Rhode Island. Their lifeless bodies would remain untouched for three and a half weeks until July 28, 1863. That afternoon, John Gardner would arrive in Gettysburg to recover the body of his half-brother, Alfred, and then hastily closed up the grave again leaving William Jones alone in the shallow hole.

There would be no funeral or eulogies for Jones. There would be no crowded churches with family mourning the loss of the young man, who was just a few months shy of his 26th birthday. Perhaps then it was fitting, that Jones would eventually be among those who were honored in one of the greatest speeches ever delivered. Four months after the battle, Jones and more than 3,000 other Union soldiers were exhumed from their temporary graves and moved to a new cemetery in Gettysburg. Pennsylvania's Governor Curtin, was outraged by the post-battle conditions and ordered a cemetery to be established, the Soldiers National Cemetery. The body of William Jones was exhumed for $1.59 and gently placed in a fresh pine coffin. Burial workers nailed the rough wooden marker bearing his name and rank to the top of his coffin and transported his decaying body up Taneytown Road to his final resting place. His remains were placed in the Rhode Island plot three feet deep and side by side with those who also fell from the State of Rhode Island. On the afternoon of Thursday, November 19, 1863, President Abraham Lincoln eloquently delivered his dedication remarks not too distant from where the body of William Jones was ultimately laid to rest. Lincoln's eloquent address called on the nation to remember those devoted soldiers who fought, struggled, and died so that the splintered country could be made whole.

Calvin Macomber

The only living relative of William Jones, his mother Margaret Nott, did not know the fate of her only son. There was never any mention of a John Mahoney who was killed at Gettysburg. In the years after the war, Margaret's second husband died and her four stepchildren moved away. She was once again faced with economic hardship and poverty. Many years after the war, veterans of the Battery B Veteran Association contacted her and relayed the sad news of her son's death. She filed a military pension in her son's name but struggled to prove to the Pension Office that William Jones of Providence was actually John Mahoney of Boston. Battery B veterans assisted the elderly and grieving mother testifying that John Mahoney and William Jones were the same person. She would eventually receive her son's service pension 27 years later on July 22, 1890.

Our Story

In 1908, John Mowry wrote a letter to the Battery B Veteran Association recalling the harrowing events of July 3, 1863. In his note, he wrote that in a rare sequence of events, the limber chest belonging to the fourth gun, where Jones and Gardner were killed was eventually brought to the rear and placed in the artillery reserve. One of the former Battery B officers, George W. Adams, recognized the book that Jones had placed in the limber before he was killed and saved it from being destroyed. Adams held onto the book and eventually sent it to John Mowry almost 45 years later as a symbol of remembrance from that awful afternoon.

Two years later in 1910, John Mowry, John Delevan, Charles Paine, and other surviving members of the Battery B Veteran Association dedicated their 49th Battery B reunion to the memory of their fallen friend and comrade. The name John Mahoney would be lost to history. Instead, the man who bravely stood in the face of death would forever be remembered as William Jones.

Pension File granted to John Mahoney's mother, Margaret Nott in 1890

Grave of John Mahoney (William Jones), Soldiers National Cemetery, Gettysburg, Pennsylvania

Notes:
1. John H. Rhodes, *The History of Battery B, First Regiment Rhode Island Light Artillery* (Providence: Snow and Farnum, Printers, 1894) 209-214, 368
2. Jeffrey Martin, "William Jones," Killed at Gettysburg: The Final Footsteps of Gettysburg's Fallen<http://www.killedatgettysburg.org> (Civil War Institute at Gettysburg College), 2017. [Accessed October 15, 2020)
3. https://www.washingtonpost.com/local/after-1863-battle-of-gettysburg-a-grisly-but-noble-enterprise-to-honor-the-fallen/2013/09/12/769c47e6-163c-11e3-a2ec-b47e45e6f8ef_story.html
4. Battery B First Rhode Island Light Artillery July 2nd & 3rd, A presentation at Gettysburg, Corporal John Delevan
5. Mowry, John. Letter to Charles Tillinghast Straight. 28 March 1908. Battery B First Rhode Island Light Artillery Inc. Collection
6. Steven Howell, Corp. William Jones, Find a Grave. https://www.findagrave.com/cgibin/fg.cgi?page=gr&GSln=Jones&GSfn=William&GSbyrel=all&GSdyrel=all&GSst=40&GScnty=2241&GScntry=4&GSob=n&GRid=5903857&df=all&
7. Case Files of Organization Index to Pension Files of Veterans Who Served Between 1861-1900, Jones, William (NARA ARC 258825) FOLD3 Digital Source
8. All photos courtesy of Battery B First Rhode Island Light Artillery Inc. Collection

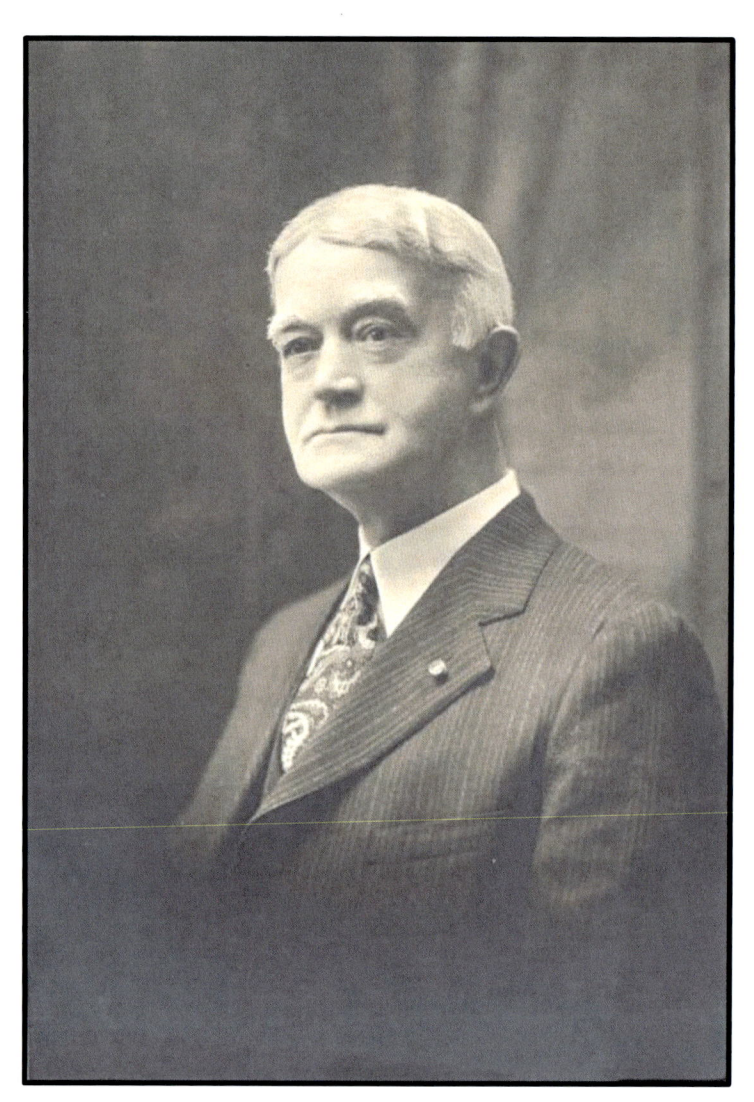

CHARLES TILLINGHAST STRAIGHT

40

A Beloved Son

Charles Tillinghast Straight was understandably surprised when Battery B veteran John Holland, stood up at the end of the annual Battery B meeting and handed him a magnificently engraved silver cup with an inscription that read: *"Presented to Charles Tillinghast Straight by members and comrades of Battery B First Rhode Island Light Artillery Veteran Association at its Forty-First Reunion August Thirteen Nineteen Hundred Ten."* After all, Charles was not a member of Battery B, never fought in a battle, and was only a year old when the Civil War began. Still, the surviving members of the Battery B Veteran Association were indebted to him for his unwavering dedication to their organization and the history they strived to preserve. Humbled and grateful, Charles Tillinghast Straight accepted the gift as best he could in honor of the father he never knew.

Charles Tillinghast Straight was born on October 27, 1860, in West Greenwich, Rhode Island. He was the second child of Albert Aaron Straight and Angeline Avery Tillinghast Straight. When he was a week old, his mother died of complications from childbirth. Before his first birthday, his father enlisted in the Federal Army and served as a Sergeant with Battery B First Rhode Island Light Artillery. Sergeant Albert Straight served for two years before dying in the service of the Union cause on November 16, 1863. Orphaned as a baby, Charles was placed in the care of his maternal grandparents, John and Susan Tillinghast. His older sister, Laura Amanda Straight, would be sent to live with her paternal grandparents, Aaron and Abigail Straight. Both children would grow up never knowing their mother or father.

Charles Tillinghast Straight would go on to marry Ella Horton Straight. Together they had one daughter, Louella Tillinghast Straight who was born January 28, 1899. They lived in Pawtucket, Rhode Island, where Charles worked for the United States Postal Service and later worked for the Pawtucket Water Department in the early 1900s. Always curious and proud of his father's service during the Civil War, Charles spent much of his life trying to gather as much information about his deceased father, Albert Straight. In the process, he wrote hundreds of letters to surviving veterans of Battery B First Rhode Island Light Artillery. In his letters, he asked veterans to share their experiences about Battery B, especially those experiences that would shed light on his father and his service in the Union Artillery. In 1904, Charles was elected Secretary and Treasurer of the Battery B First Rhode Island Veteran Association. He inherited a list of 50 individuals of the Battery both dead and living.

Knowing that there had to be many more surviving members, Straight wrote to every postmaster, Grand Army Post, and the United States Postal Service in search of surviving veterans. Through his efforts, he increased the rolls of known Battery B veterans threefold, bringing the total to 150 members, many of them by this time, living outside of New England. Straight wrote continuously to the numerous Battery B veterans and their family members from 1904 through the early 1920s. Through his correspondence, visits, and meetings with Battery B veterans and surviving relatives, he is essentially responsible for preserving much of the historical information, stories, biographies, photos, and original items of Battery B First Rhode Island Light Artillery. He traveled to Gettysburg multiple times

Ella Horton Straight

and stood in the very place where his father heroically commanded the now-famous *"Gettysburg Gun."* He kept meticulous notes of each of the annual meetings including the nomination of officers, finances, deaths, and historical anniversaries.

He attended all of the Battery B annual reunions at Boyden Heights, Crescent Park and Duby's Grove from August of 1904 until the last reunion in 1923. That year, there were only 15 Battery B members alive and only two lived in Rhode Island at the time. He was beloved by all of the veterans who talked to him warmly of his father's leadership, service, and dedication to the Battery. In 1910, the Battery B veterans surprised him with the presentation of an engraved silver cup in honor of his service to the association. On one side was an engraving of his father's gun, with the solid shot still in the muzzle. On the other side was an inscription crowned with the trifold of the 2nd Corps. It was an emotional tribute to the man who spent his life honoring his father's legacy, Sergeant Straight, and who in turn, gained the love and respect of so many men who adopted him as their own. The day after receiving this gift, Charles wrote a letter to Colonel Thomas Fred Brown of Battery B. *"The Association presented me with a very handsome and costly loving cup. It was a perfect surprise to me as I never had heard the first thing about it...To tell you I appreciate this token far more than mere words can express is only telling the plain truth: I do not deserve it. For I have only tried to do my duty and make the Association fill its proper mission. And keep the members in close touch. Over and over again I have told them I was not of them - could not be by any possible stretch of imagination. I am one removed. I also said I did not need the visible token to assure me I had their respect and affection. For in the hearty hand clasp the kindly word I KNOW I have their confidence and esteem. I am deeply sensible of the great honor conferred, and it will be my pleasure to treasure this mark of their good will*

Cup presented to Charles Tillinghast Straight from surviving Battery B members

as long as my home shall endure." As the years rolled on and Battery B veterans passed away, Charles Straight sent a silk American flag to each of the grieving families as a tribute from the Veteran Association. He came to know and love the veterans as his own, so much so, that he could not bring himself to attend any of their funerals.

In addition to being an associate member of the Battery B Veteran Association, Charles was also an active member of the Rhode Island Society of the Sons of the American Revolution and a member of the Connecticut Society of the War of 1812 where he carried on the legacy of his maternal Tillinghast lineage who fought in the Revolutionary War and the War of 1812. Charles Tillinghast Straight passed away on April 17, 1940, at the age of 79 in Pawtucket, Rhode Island. His wife, Ella, would pass away two years later in 1942. They are buried at Oak Grove Cemetery, Pawtucket, Rhode Island.

Louella Tillinghast Straight.

Charles Tillinghast Straight headstone at Oak Grove Cemetery, Pawtucket, Rhode Island

Notes:
1. Battery B Meeting Notes, courtesy of Battery B First Rhode Island Light Artillery Inc. Collection
2. Letter from Charles Tillinghast Straight to Lewis D. Blake dated December 4, 1927, courtesy of Battery B First Rhode Island Light Artillery, Inc. Collection
3. Letter from Charles Tillinghast Straight to Colonel Fred Brown dated August 14, 1910, courtesy of Battery B First Rhode Island Light Artillery Inc. Collection
4. Silver Cup Photo courtesy of Phil and Mary DiMaria Collection
5. All photos courtesy of Battery B First Rhode Island Light Artillery Inc. Collection

Battery B First Rhode Island Light Artillery Reunion, Boyden Heights, Rhode Island (August 18, 1908)

EPILOGUE

On August 13, 1870, five years after the Battery's guns fell silent, the surviving members of Battery B gathered at Rocky Point, Rhode Island, for their first annual reunion. On that day, they formed the First Rhode Island Battery B Veteran Association. Over the little more than five decades that followed, the members of the Battery B Veteran Association would meet yearly to honor the historic day when Battery B was mustered into the United States service.

The veterans and their families gathered at places like Ocean Cottage, Silver Spring, Crescent Park, Rocky Point, and Boyden Heights. In peace as in war, they worked together to record and publish their regimental history, honor fallen comrades, preserve their historic artillery piece, the *Gettysburg Gun*, and erect a monument at Gettysburg, dedicated to the sacrifice of those who struggled and died there. They elected officers, took formal meeting notes, and collected dues. But most of all, the members of the Veteran Association, gathered each year to simply be with one another. They understood the silent bond that existed between them. That bond, forged in war and cherished in peace, was one of camaraderie, friendship, and service. As the years rolled on, the number of Battery B veterans in attendance at the reunions dwindled. Increasing age, ongoing health issues, and distance, prohibited many of the men from attending these events. In 1923, though they were unaware of it at the time, the veterans would meet for their last annual reunion in Danielson, Connecticut. In May 1924, when the President of the Veteran Association, Amos Horton Armington passed away, and with only 10 Battery B veterans still able to attend, they voted not to hold another reunion. The last remaining veteran of Battery B, James Blade, died in 1938 at the age of 96. His passing marked the end of an era but, it did not mark the end of Battery B.

Battery B as a fighting unit, would go on to provide support in the Spanish American War. During World War I, they would sail for France and fight in the trenches as part of the One Hundred Third Field Artillery, Twenty-Sixth Division. Nearly 125 years after the Civil War, Battery B First Rhode Island Light Artillery was reactivated on May 8, 1986, by Rhode Island Governor, Edward DiPrete.

Today, Battery B First Rhode Island Light Artillery Inc., operates under the original Rhode Island Historic Military Command and is considered part of the 103rd Field Artillery Division, who trace their lineage back to Battery B's service during the Civil War. Members of the modern-day Battery act as custodians of the original Battery's history, service, and sacrifice. In 2004, Battery B presented the Battery's guidon to soldiers of the 103rd Field Artillery on their way to be deployed to Iraq and Afghanistan.

In an act of solidarity, soldiers of the 103rd brought the flag with them to Iraq and proudly flew it at their field camp headquarters.

Like that flag flapping in the breeze, the stories of those who served in Battery B First Rhode Island Light Artillery ripple and undulate across the many decades and touch our hearts. Their stories, telling us who they were, in turn, teach us much about ourselves, our shared humanity and our common desire for unity and peace.

Members of the 103rd Field Artillery hoist the Battery B guidon in Iraq

Members of Battery B First Rhode Island Light Artillery Inc, Gettysburg
July 21, 2019
(Photo by Rob Gibson)

Our Story

The Gettysburg Gun, July 3, 1863.

ACKNOWLEDGEMENTS

With heartfelt gratitude to Phil DiMaria for his unwavering support and guidance, without whom this book would not be possible. Special thanks to Barbara Laird for helping to edit this book with her careful and kind attention to detail.

Lastly, my profound thanks (always) to my wife, Adriana, and to my daughter and son, Sophia and Nicholas, for their love and for believing in my dream to write this book.

ABOUT THE AUTHOR

Stephen G. Evangelista is a native New Englander who grew up in Johnston, Rhode Island. He is a graduate of Providence College and serves as a member of the Senior Executive Service Corps in the United States Federal Government. He is a keen historian and member of the reactivated Battery B First Rhode Island Light Artillery. He lives in Maryland with his wife and two children.

For more information visit evangelistabooks.com.

Made in the USA
Monee, IL
10 May 2021